Penny Ur's 100 Teaching Tips

Cambridge Handbooks for Language Teachers

This series, now with over 50 titles, offers practical ideas, techniques and activities for the teaching of English and other languages, providing inspiration for both teachers and trainers.

The Pocket Editions come in a handy, pocket-sized format and are crammed full of tips and ideas from experienced English language teaching professionals, to enrich your teaching practice.

Recent titles in this series:

Grammar Practice Activities (Second edition)
A practical guide for teachers
PENNY UR

Vocabulary Activities
PENNY UR

Classroom Management Techniques
JIM SCRIVENER

CLIL Activities
A resource for subject and language teachers
LIZ DALE AND ROSIE TANNER

Language Learning with Technology
Ideas for integrating technology in the classroom
GRAHAM STANLEY

Translation and Own-language Activities
PHILIP KERR

Language Learning with Digital Video
BEN GOLDSTEIN AND PAUL DRIVER

Discussions and More
Oral fluency practice in the classroom
PENNY UR

Penny Ur's 100 Teaching Tips

Penny Ur

Consultant and editor: Scott Thornbury

CAMBRIDGE
UNIVERSITY PRESS

CAMBRIDGE
UNIVERSITY PRESS

University Printing House, Cambridge CB2 8BS, United Kingdom

Cambridge University Press is part of the University of Cambridge.

It furthers the University's mission by disseminating knowledge in the pursuit of education, learning and research at the highest international levels of excellence.

www.cambridge.org
Information on this title: www.cambridge.org/9781316507285

First published 2016

A catalogue record for this publication is available from the British Library

ISBN 978-1-316-50728-5 Paperback
ISBN 978-1-316-50729-2 Apple iBook
ISBN 978-1-316-50730-8 Google ebook
ISBN 978-1-316-50731-5 Kindle ebook
ISBN 978-1-316-50732-2 eBooks.com ebook

Contents

Why I wrote this book

English teachers in the course of their teaching careers accumulate a wealth of practical know-how about classroom teaching. But few of them publish this knowledge – mainly because they simply don't have the time. (There are, of course, websites with teaching guidance of one kind or another, though many of these are not very practical, and it takes a lot of surfing to find good ones.) So an enormous number of experienced-based insights discovered by expert teachers in the course of their teaching careers are lost as far as future generations of teachers are concerned. The result is that many new teachers find themselves laboriously 're-inventing the wheel', or discovering a useful teaching idea much too late, when they could have shortened the process by learning from their predecessors. ('Why did nobody tell me...?!')

So having myself retired from school teaching – though I still teach academic English to adults – it seemed a good idea to write my own set of practical tips, from which other teachers might benefit.

I started teaching English in a primary school in Israel in 1968. It was a fairly discouraging experience at first, with lots of discipline problems and misunderstandings, since I didn't know my students' language very well, and wasn't familiar with the culture. I remember telling a colleague at the end of my first year that I didn't think I should continue because I was clearly not suited to English teaching. He told me to stop thinking so much about my own problems and look at my students: ask myself whether they were learning from my lessons, and whether they were motivated to continue learning. If they were, he said, I was a successful teacher and should continue. So I did, and I did. I suppose this is my first and perhaps most basic tip: don't worry so much about yourself and your teaching, look at the students, and what and how they are learning. Anyhow, I went on to teach English in primary and secondary classes in State schools – with some breaks to teach university courses or to study – until I retired in 2006. I must have clocked up thousands of hours of classroom teaching. My professional knowledge derives primarily from that experience, and is the basis of the tips in this book.

I suggest you don't try to read straight through the book, but rather browse through it looking for headings that interest you. The topics are listed alphabetically, each followed by a set of associated tips. (If you don't find the topic you want, try the Index.) Each tip appears at the top of a page, followed by comments which include personal anecdotes, examples of classroom procedures, references to research or internet sources or anything else I thought you might find interesting or helpful.

Some of the ideas may be familiar; others you may have come across in the past but need to be reminded of; yet others may be quite new. In any case, be aware that not all may be right for you. My professional experience is, obviously, based on my own situation and yours may be quite different, as may your teaching personality and the character and expectations of your students. So you may find you need to modify or adapt some of the tips, or even completely reject them. Please don't regard them as directives from an authority, but as suggestions from a colleague: use them selectively and critically.

With this reservation in mind, read on. I hope that you will find enough interesting and useful teaching ideas to make your reading worthwhile.

Beginning and ending the lesson

Teacher courses often include a unit on 'lesson-planning', which relates mostly to the selection of the lesson components, and how these will be ordered. But it's important also to think about how you'll 'frame' the lesson with effective beginnings and endings.

1   Start with a smile
2   Begin and end clearly
3   Give an advance overview
4   Teach new material first: review later
5   Don't give homework at the end
6   End with something nice

1 Start with a smile

> It is important to make eye-contact with your students and smile as you greet them at the beginning of the lesson.

In my early years of teaching I was a bit scared of my students, and was tense and serious at the beginning of lessons. In retrospect, it took me far too long to learn to relax and smile – but it made a huge difference when I did. Don't be put off if some of the students don't respond; most of them will. And remember: a serious or neutral expression on your face does not convey a neutral message – it conveys a negative one ('I'm here because I have to be, not because I have the slightest pleasure in teaching you!'), which can be easily be changed by a smile.

Non-verbal communication, including facial expression, body language and gesture, plays a key role in maintaining your relationship with the students in a class. It does not, as a popular myth would have it, convey 50% or more of the actual messages coming across in a conversation, but it's still important. Try searching online for the phrase "non-verbal communication" and you'll find a lot of very useful guidance. Most of the websites relate to personal relationships in the context of employment in general, but can be readily applied to classroom interaction.

Note, however, that the smile can also be over-used. The recommendation to smile at the beginning of the lesson does not mean that you have to smile all the way through it. How much you do so of course depends largely on your own personality: some of us are more smiley than others! But remember that, like constant, indiscriminate praise, smiles that are over-used lose their impact. Use a smile to respond to a student's successful or amusing contribution; or, together with a favourable comment at the end of an activity, to provide the class with a brief but welcome break from the effort of concentrating on serious learning tasks.

P.S. Smile at the end of the lesson too! (See Tip 6.)

Begin and end clearly   2

> There should be a definite moment when the lesson
> begins: a dividing line between 'not lesson' and 'lesson'.
> And similarly, there should be a clear point when it ends.

So before you start, allow the students a couple of minutes to get organized, sit down, take out any necessary books, pens, laptops, whatever. You'll need this time to get organised yourself: get ready any materials or equipment you are going to need, check attendance. Then give a clear signal that the lesson is beginning: this could be a simple verbal announcement: 'OK, quiet please, we'll begin the lesson with …' or possibly a bell or a buzzer. Otherwise you might find yourself with a slow 'creeping start' where some students gradually start paying attention while others are still talking to each other. In such cases the lesson beginning is uneasy and blurred, and you'll find yourself wasting time repeating instructions.

The same applies to the end of the lesson. You need a clear signal that the lesson is over. It's a good idea to do some kind of rounding-off: a recap of what has been done, followed by a stock farewell phrase like 'OK, see you on (whenever the next lesson is), have a good day!' (see Tip 6).

Rituals can help a lot here: these are routine procedures that may or may not be meaningful in themselves, but function chiefly as attention-catching symbols of some event or transition. For example, in many countries the national anthem is sung at the beginning or end of national events. In younger classes, the opening ritual may take the form of the writing of the date on the board; a song or a chant; chorused exchanges such as 'How are you today?' – 'Fine, thank you!'. With more advanced classes, the opening may be signalled by semi-ritualized procedures such as a brief student- or teacher-initiated presentation of a 'Word of the Day'; or an announcement of the programme of the present session (see Tip 3).

3 Give an advance overview

Particularly with teenage and adult groups, it's important to provide the class at the beginning with information about what's planned for the lesson.

You can just tell your students what you're going to do; or have the programme written up before you start; or write it up as you tell them. I usually go for the third option. Students like knowing the plan: it gives them a reassuring sense that they know where they are going, and helps to keep the lesson process orderly and purposeful. If you like, you can also include an item labelled 'if we have time', to allow yourself flexibility of timing. Occasionally, of course, the lesson takes an unexpected turn, so you decide to go with the flow, and don't get to complete most of the plan. Even in such cases, giving a provisional plan in advance is a good idea, for the reasons given above. You can always use the missed bits in later lessons.

Some proponents of a learner-centred approach suggest that you should not pre-plan, but let the students take most of the decisions as to what happens in the lesson. I don't agree. Being learner-centred does not mean passing the responsibility for lesson-planning to the students. The classroom is not a democracy, as it has often, and rightly, been said. (Try searching online for this sentence in double quotation marks and see how many hits you get!) Students would not learn very much if they had also to work on planning the content or process of lessons; and it is part of the teacher's professional responsibility to take these kinds of decisions. But you should also make such decisions clear to the students before implementing them. This is partly a matter of professional respect and consideration, and partly because, as discussed above, advance organisers help create a sense of confidence and purpose.

Teach new material first: review later **4**

> In principle, teach new or more difficult material early in
> the lesson, when students are at their freshest. Then go
> back and do a quick review of it at the end of the lesson,
> after you have spent time doing other things.

Difficult texts or tasks usually need to be planned for early in the
lesson when students are likely to have more mental energy than later
on. Similarly, new items are remembered better if they are taught first
at the beginning of the lesson and then practised at a later stage. In
principle, we learn things best if we review them little and often rather
than in one long solid stretch. This is called the principle of *distributed
practice* as contrasted with *massed practice* (see the reference below).
So if, for example, you have some new vocabulary to teach, do so
for a few minutes at the beginning, then do other activities, such as
communicative tasks, or reading comprehension, in the main part of
your lesson. Then come back to the new vocabulary at the end to do
another five-minute review. This will result in much better learning than
if you had done a solid ten-minute session of vocabulary teaching at the
beginning.

But that isn't all. Distributed practice can be made even more effective if
it is implemented using the principle of *expanding rehearsal* (again see
the reference below). This means that the first time you teach something
new, you review it fairly soon after the first encounter – say, later in
the same lesson, as suggested here. Then the next time widen the gap.
So you might review again the following day, or a couple of days later,
whenever the next lesson takes place. Then perhaps wait four or five
days until the next time; and then a week; then two or three weeks …
and so on.

Baddeley, A. (1997). *Human memory: Theory and practice* (pp.156–158). Hove:
Psychology Press.

5 Don't give homework at the end

> If you know you have a homework assignment to give,
> explain it sometime in the middle of the lesson and make
> sure students have noted it down. Don't leave it until the
> last minute.

In most lessons I've observed, the teacher gives the homework last thing before the end of the lesson. It seems to be a conventional routine in lessons in all subjects, not just English. I suppose there's a kind of logic to it: we've finished the lesson, the next thing you'll do is homework, so let's give it when the lesson is over.

But in fact it's not a good idea, for various reasons. Attention is likely in general to be lower at the end of the session. Students may be packing up and not listening to you; you may not have enough time to explain properly; and the overall message is likely to be 'homework is an afterthought, not so important'. So it's much better to give it earlier. In general, give the homework immediately after the lesson component that it relates to: for example, comprehension work on a text you've been reading. Then you aren't rushed, can explain fully and answer questions about it, and students have time to write it down. If you note it at the side of the board as you explain, then you can use this note as the basis for a brief reminder before closing the lesson later.

Of course, there may be exceptions (as with any of the tips in this book!). For example, the activity that is the basis for the homework might have come at the end of the lesson anyway. Or the whole lesson might have been taken up with one ongoing activity, with no gap when you could have given homework earlier.

(For more ideas on homework giving and checking, see Tips 44–49.)

End with something nice   6

> Just before closing the lesson, try to find something
> pleasant to do or say so that your students leave the
> classroom with a smile.

Some ideas are:

- a funny story or joke;
- a compliment (if it has been earned!) on what the students have managed to do this lesson, or on their behaviour;
- a new website you've come across that might interest them;
- an interesting fact about English;
- congratulations on an achievement of one of the students;
- singing Happy Birthday to someone with a birthday.

You don't want to spend too much time on such things, obviously, or too much effort preparing or planning them. And don't feel you have to do them every lesson. But a 'smiley' ending is something to bear in mind and to do when you can.

Apropos telling jokes: yes, students like teachers with a sense of humour, and there is some evidence that humour, if used appropriately, can improve learning. But for many of us, that's not as easy as it sounds. It's difficult to find a set of jokes that can be told in English that is simple enough for our class to understand (though see the reference below for some ideas). And even if we know the jokes, how good are we at telling them? If you are good at telling jokes, great! If (like me) you aren't so good at it, be comforted that many excellent teachers are not particularly entertaining. (I'm sure you can remember examples from your school days.) The ability to tell jokes is certainly far from being an essential teacher quality: it's just a nice optional extra. And there are lots of other options, as shown above, for ending the lesson with a smile.

Medgyes, P. (2002). *Laughing matters: Humour in the language classroom*. Cambridge: Cambridge University Press.

The Coursebook

A good coursebook is often an essential basis of the course content, and can make a real contribution to successful learning. But it needs to be used critically and selectively, not just followed page by page.

7   Use the coursebook – selectively

8   Vary the way you use exercises

9   Allow lots of right answers

10   Recycle tasks

Use the coursebook – selectively   7

The coursebook is a valuable tool, but that doesn't mean you have to use all of it. Choose in advance what you feel is essential to get through, and what can be skipped if you don't have enough time.

Some writers have suggested that we shouldn't use coursebooks, on the grounds that they de-skill and disempower the teacher and deny us the right to teach creatively. But in fact it's a useful – or even essential – tool for most of us. I certainly needed one. I didn't have the time to find my own texts or exercises or plan my own course programme. On the other hand, using the coursebook doesn't mean going through it page by page doing everything the writers provide. There are bound to be bits you don't like so much. Maybe the content of a text isn't suitable for your students; maybe it's just boring; maybe you just can't see how a task would work in your classroom; maybe there's just too much of it.

Anyhow, the main tip here is to take the time to look through the book at the beginning of the course and note for yourself what you're definitely going to use, what you definitely aren't, and what you may use if you have time. Do the same, in more detail, at the beginning of each unit. If you don't, you might find later that you have to skip some really nice bits, or aren't teaching some tasks or texts thoroughly enough, simply because you've run out of time.

Sometimes you can get your students to help you. Ask them to look forward through the unit (or the entire book) and tell you which bits they are more, or less, interested in doing. It's a good way of giving them a preview of the material and can help you make decisions as to what to prioritize.

8 Vary the way you use exercises

The usual way to do coursebook exercises in class is the classic teacher-student 'ping-pong'. The teacher asks 'Who can answer number one?', students raise their hands, the teacher nominates a student to answer, and then corrects or approves their response. But there are lots of other ways to do them.

The conventional kind of question-answer interaction described above has several drawbacks. It's slow; it only directly involves one student at a time; other students might get bored; and students who don't raise their hands may not be attending at all. Occasionally coursebooks suggest other options; more often they don't. Here are some ideas:

- Let students do the 'ping-pong' in small groups, with one of them role-playing the teacher. They ask you for help only if they're not sure of an answer.
- Students do the exercise in pairs, orally or in writing.
- Students do the exercise individually in writing.
- Students do as much as they can of the exercise in writing, within, say, five minutes (either individually or in pairs).

As they are working, move around the classroom to help or monitor. Later, if you feel necessary, you can check their answers through the usual 'ping-pong' – but then it goes very fast, as the students have already prepared the answers. Alternatively, just tell students the answers (or write them up on the board) and get them to self-check.

The main advantage of the types of interaction suggested in the bulleted points above is that far more students participate so they are likely to be more involved and learn more. The disadvantage is that they're a bit more tricky to organize – but that's only true the first couple of times you do it. Once students are used to the different options, they move into them quickly and smoothly.

Allow lots of right answers

Most coursebook grammar and vocabulary exercises are 'closed ended': there's one right answer for each item. But it's easy to change them so that lots of right answers are possible, making the exercise available to many more levels of student, as well as more interesting and fun to do.

For example: if you have a set of questions like the following:

Write the sentence in the past:

She ... at six o'clock. (leave).

Tell the students to ignore the verb in brackets and suggest any verb they like in the past: *came, spoke, woke* ... . Or leave the verb, and delete the end of the sentence (*at six o'clock*); then invite the students to create their own continuations after *left*: 'She left London', 'left the school', 'left her husband' ... .

Similarly, if you have gap-fills which depend on a bank of items (*Complete the sentence using one of the words from the box*), tell students to ignore the bank and think of a variety of possibilities for each gap. Or if you have a matching exercise, delete one of the columns of 'matches' and invite students to invent their own match for each item in the remaining column.

Teachers sometimes think that if you make items open-ended like this then they are more difficult; but this isn't necessarily true. If students understand and can do the exercise in its original form – i.e. its language is not too difficult – then they can certainly do the variations, since these will be based on language they know.

So the basic principle is to delete the words that determine what the 'one right answer' has to be, and allow students to insert their own. Try it! The results are often entertaining, as well as providing a lot more opportunities for practice of the target item(s).

10 Recycle tasks

> A good coursebook task is often worth recycling, to give further opportunities for review and to reinforce the language learnt. But you sometimes need to do it slightly differently the second time, to add challenge and make sure students aren't bored.

It's a bit of a waste to use each task only once if it's a good one, and there's plenty of research to show that repeated reading or repetition of a task leads to better learning. (If you are interested in the evidence, have a look at the references below.) With adult classes, you can often take students into your confidence and explain frankly that we're going to repeat the task or text for the sake of the review and consolidation; and the second time round usually goes much faster, so they don't have time to get bored. With younger or less motivated learners you'll need to think about how to make the repetition interesting. You might:

- tell students to do a pair activity again with a different partner;
- ask students to close their books, and write down as much as they can remember of the exercise or text;
- tell students to do the exercise again for homework;
- tell students to do the exercise or text again, but inserting one new word in each sentence, without changing the meaning too much;
- do the same, but changing one word in each sentence;
- do the same, but deleting one word in each sentence;
- do the exercise again but making it open-ended (see Tip 9).

Gorsuch, G., & Taguchi, E. (2010). Developing reading fluency and comprehension using repeated reading: Evidence from longitudinal student reports. *Language Teaching Research*, 14(1), 27–60.

Lynch, T. & J. Maclean. (2000). Exploring the benefits of task repetition and recycling for classroom language learning. *Language Teaching Research*, 4(3), 21.

Discipline

Maintaining order in the classroom is probably the single biggest problem for most novice teachers. I know it was mine. Normally you'll get better at it as you become more experienced; but there are some fairly simple strategies which can also help.

11 Learn students' names

12 Keep the lesson moving

13 Make the lesson interesting

14 Catch problems as they start

15 Avoid confrontations

16 Compliment good behaviour

11 Learn students' names

> Knowing students' names not only conveys the message that you care about them as individuals, but also enables you to respond to them personally if there are any problems.

Learning names can be difficult, particularly if the class is large. Some teachers get the students to write their names on cards and display them on their clothes or on their desks, or have the names shown on a clearly visible fixed seating plan. But I prefer to do without these, because if I use them I find myself relying on the cards or plan and not making the effort to learn the names myself.

So my recommendation is to try to learn students' names through direct name-learning procedures. In the first lesson I ask students to introduce themselves, after which I test myself. I tell them 'You are…', when I remember who they are, and ask them to remind me when I don't. At times during the first few lessons when the students are busy on individual or group work, I look round the class and try to recall names. It also helps to note on my class list brief characteristics of students' appearance or behaviour that may serve as reminders: hair-style, eye-colour, whatever. And I find it a useful routine to test myself publicly on names at the beginning of the first few lessons. I name each student in turn, or ask them to remind me. Believe me, it's worth investing the time and students appreciate that you are making the effort to get to know them.

If the students don't already know each other, then some ice-breaking activities can also help. For example, ask them to mill around and meet each other, exchanging personal information; you can also participate. Then sit with the students in a circle, and each participant introduces someone they've just met, including personal information: 'Her name is Lena and she likes Italian food'.

Keep the lesson moving   12

> The more fully occupied the students are in purposeful learning activity, the more likely they are to cooperate and work well. Boredom is a key cause of discipline problems.

A major principle in dealing with problems of classroom discipline is to prevent them arising in the first place. Keeping the momentum going during a lesson is one key way to do this.

First, you need a fully-planned lesson, a complete programme of activities and tasks for the entire period, so that you know at any point what's coming next. A gap while you consider what to do next is likely to produce discipline problems: not only because students get bored, but also because of the uneasy feeling that there is no clear plan, or that the teacher is uncertain and lacking confidence. I usually glance through my lesson notes just before I start so I can remember most of what I'd planned to do by heart and don't need to pause to refer to them very much during the lesson itself.

Second, stop longer activities as soon as you see signs that the momentum is lost and that students are losing interest and patience – even if it means postponing the ending to another lesson. This is particularly true of group work, but applies, in principle, to teacher-led or individual activities as well. It's better to stop while students are still interested than to insist on completing something when most of them are tired of it and want to move on to something else.

Third, prepare a reserve activity, so that if something takes less time than you thought it would (or you need to halt a longer activity earlier than you'd planned, as suggested above), you can continue seamlessly to something else without showing that you were left with an unplanned gap. A repertoire of quick activities requiring no preparation helps a lot here (see the reference below).

Ur, P., & Wright, A. (1991) *Five-minute activities*. Cambridge: Cambridge University Press.

13 Make the lesson interesting

> If students are interested in what they are doing, they are more likely to stay on-task and discipline problems will lessen or disappear.

A colleague of mine had a charismatic, authoritative personality that enabled her to control classes effortlessly. She walked into a classroom and the students immediately quietened down and waited for her to speak. She wasn't unpopular, and she wasn't unpleasantly bossy – she just had natural authority. I don't know how she did it: neither did she.

Most of us have met teachers like this, either as students ourselves or among our colleagues. But I didn't – and still don't – have this quality of natural authority. I learned, as we all do, a lot of useful classroom management techniques (see Jim Scrivener's excellent book referred to below) but without doubt my main means of dealing with potentially undisciplined classes was by keeping them interested in what they were doing. And I spent a lot of preparation time looking for interesting visual materials in colour magazines, for example (this was before the internet, remember!), or thinking of how to make repetitive activities more game-like and fun to do (see Tips 21–25). And it worked.

I have some more detailed ideas later in this book (see Tips 50–55) about effective and perhaps less well-known techniques for raising and maintaining interest in the classroom, but here are some important basic ones to be going on with:

- Plan your lesson to include a number of shorter and varied activities.
- Use pictures or other visuals to back up texts or tasks.
- Use activities that involve all, or most of, the students at once.
- Use games, provided these are learning-rich.
- Personalize: make opportunities for students to relate to their own tastes, experiences, etc.

Scrivener, J. (2012). *Classroom management techniques*. Cambridge: Cambridge University Press.

Catch problems as they start

> Don't ignore minor discipline problems thinking they'll go away by themselves. They usually won't.

It's all too easy to deliberately ignore small, not-too-obvious problems that are just starting: two students, for example, who begin chatting quietly at the back of the class. You're busy dealing with the ongoing lesson process, the disturbance isn't too bad. Hopefully, you think, they'll eventually stop talking on their own and return to the current task, I'll just ignore them. This was my response to this kind of situation hundreds of times when I started teaching, and I learned the hard way that it was a mistake. Nine times out of ten, such problems don't go away on their own. On the contrary, the disturbing students provide an example for others, who see that they are continuing without any reaction from you and are encouraged to imitate them. React quickly – as soon as you notice the problem – and firmly. Sometimes this can be done silently: by stopping and waiting, and making eye contact with the inattentive students; by moving to stand near them; or by gesture. Sometimes you actually need to say something: a quick request, polite but assertive. In any case – don't ignore the problem!

It's relatively easy to deal with minor problems like these that have only just begun. It becomes much more difficult if they have been going on for a while, or have begun to escalate. And the fact that you react quickly also makes it clear to students that you are constantly aware of all of them and what they are doing.

By the way, note that I wrote above that problems don't go away 'nine times out of ten', and this is a good time to mention a key maxim in classroom teaching: 'Never say never'. Any tip, any principle, however true and valid, has its exceptions. Sometimes the disturbers do quieten down on their own and return to the task. But not very often.

15 Avoid confrontations

Try not to get into public confrontation in class with a student or group of students who are creating problems. It can waste a lot of valuable lesson time and rarely leads to good solutions.

Some students – particularly teenagers – can sometimes get aggressive over issues like too much homework or some task they don't like, and try to get you to engage in a public argument with them. Don't.

If the conflict is with a particular individual student, then set up a time to meet him or her privately, and sort out the problem without an audience of other members of the class. If it is a whole-class issue, then there are basically three options:

One: insist immediately and firmly on what you've decided and move on.

Two: give in, if you think they may be right. You won't lose face, provided that a) you do it very quickly, giving your reasons; and b) you don't do it too often!

Three: postpone. Tell them you don't want to discuss it now, but will return to the problem in the next lesson; then go on to whatever you have planned next. The time-lapse before you come back to discussing the controversial issue is vital: the students will have calmed down and will be more ready to listen to you and you will have had time to think about how you should solve the problem. So if you come to the next lesson with a reasoned argument why your requirements should be accepted, or with a fair compromise, these are more likely to be accepted. Alternatively, come without a definite solution, but perhaps with two or three options which you open for (brief) discussion, and then decide together with the students what to do. Again, the time-distance from the original confrontation will help create an atmosphere of constructive discussion of issues rather than confrontation.

Compliment good behaviour   16

By the nature of things, our attention is drawn to bad or unacceptable behaviour, and we don't tend to notice when students are working quietly or cooperatively: but we should.

We naturally notice students who chat with each other, or send text messages or play games on their mobile phones when they should be working on a learning task, those who refuse to do what they are asked, those who come late or leave early. And we may respond to such problems in ways suggested in Tips 14 and 15. As we should: it's part of our job.

But what I'm suggesting here is that we should also be aware of individual students or whole groups who are working well and draw attention to them. It's not easy to remember to do so; but it's important.

With younger classes, some teachers – in addition to complimenting individuals – use a system of stars. There's a list of dates of lessons on the classroom wall, and at the end of each lesson, if it was a good one where students worked well, the teacher compliments the class and sticks a star in the appropriate cell. If the lesson didn't go well, there is simply no star. When the class achieves a set number of stars, there is some kind of treat or reward, and/or public congratulation by the school principal.

With individuals, or older classes, it's enough to occasionally draw attention to good behaviour: with a verbal comment, either as it's happening, or at the end of the lesson (see Tip 6). Another possibility is to send a note or email to the students themselves, or to their parents. In any case, it's a nice opportunity to compliment students who may not be getting very high grades on tests, but who are working well and deserve credit for it.

Error Correction

This is a controversial topic, but on the whole the consensus today is that error correction helps learning. There are, however, occasional situations where we might prefer not to correct; and there are different ways of doing so, some more effective than others.

17 Do correct mistakes
18 Correct (sometimes) during speech
19 Get students to self-correct
20 Draw attention to right answers

Do correct mistakes 17

> **In most cases, if you're wondering whether you should or should not correct a mistake: do!**

There's quite a lot of convincing research evidence that error correction helps learning (see the overview referred to below). And most learners, if you ask them, will tell you that they want you to correct their mistakes in both speech and writing.

I remember running an interactive journal project with my students during which they recorded their entries, then I listened and recorded my responses. At the beginning, I didn't correct mistakes on the basis that what was important was the message, not the accuracy. After the first round, one of the students came and asked me to tell her if there were any mistakes in her speech in my recorded responses. I agreed, and asked if there was anyone else who also wanted me to do so. The response was a unanimous 'Yes, please!'.

This doesn't mean that you should correct every single error. There are situations where just getting the message across is the priority, and you don't need to worry about mistakes. And certainly you should not expect each correction to result in complete eradication of the mistake forever! But making mistakes and having them corrected is one major avenue through which we learn; and it should be related to as such. So if a student makes a mistake, try to treat it not as a failure, but as a learning opportunity. For example: 'Did you notice that you said "He a boy"? ... You need to remember to put in *is*: He *is* a boy' – rather than: 'You got that wrong, you should have said...'.

Lyster, R., & Saito, K. (2010). Interactional feedback as instructional input: A synthesis of classroom SLA research. *Language, Interaction and Acquisition/Langage, Interaction et Acquisition*, 1(2), 276–297.

18   Correct (sometimes) during speech

> You may have been advised never to interrupt students
> to correct when they're in the middle of speaking in a
> communication activity. But there are times when you
> can – and should.

It's true that correcting a student in the middle of their speech may
be inappropriate. It may disturb the communicative flow, and may
distract or distress the student. On the other hand, letting an error go
by without comment may contribute to its *fossilization*: the student gets
so used to making the error that it's very difficult for him or her later to
substitute the correct form. Also, there are quite a lot of students who
actually prefer to be interrupted and corrected as they are speaking,
rather than waiting and getting the feedback later.

So there's no 'always' or 'never' here. It's one of those quick decisions
that teachers are making all the time. Weigh up the pros and cons in
a rapid thought-process: if I stop the student now to correct an error,
will I do more good than harm, or more harm than good? If it's a shy
student who at last is opening his mouth and saying something, then of
course you won't want to interrupt him. If it's a confident one who talks
all the time, and is making a mistake that she should have known not to
make, you may well stop her to point it out. And there are lots of other
considerations that might rush through your mind. How interested are
the students in the content of this discussion? How much do they care
about making mistakes? Is there an upcoming exam where they'll lose
points for errors? And so on.

One thing that can help you is being aware of the students' own
preferences: it's a good idea to take a minute or two to ask them.

Get students to self-correct 19

> What we want the students to remember is the correct
> form, not the mistake; so it's a good idea either to get
> them to self-correct, or to ask them to repeat / rewrite the
> correct version after you have given it to them.

Probably the most common form of oral feedback is what's called
recast: the teacher simply says the correct version of an error which
has just been made without further comment. But there is evidence that
this is actually not very effective in getting students to notice and take
on board the correct form (see the first reference below). It appears
that it's much better if there is some process that ensures that students
have noticed that they've made a mistake and have understood what
the correct form should be (called *uptake* in the literature). Probably
the best way is to get students to self-correct; but they can't always do
this. The alternative is to ask them to say the correct version that you've
given them and show they've understood it.

The same is true for written feedback, and students themselves are
probably aware of the fact. I once asked a set of teachers in a course of
mine to do a survey of their students' preferences as regards oral and
written feedback. One of the questions in the questionnaire ran 'Do
you think it's a good thing if the teacher makes you rewrite a written
assignment after it's been corrected?' To the surprise of the teachers, a
substantial majority of the students – including some quite young ones –
said 'yes'. You might try asking your own students and see what they
say. (If you're interested in looking at other findings from this survey,
see the second reference below.)

Lyster, R. & Ranta, L. (1997). Corrective feedback and learner uptake: Negotiation of
form in communicative classrooms. *Studies in Second Language Acquisition*, 19, 37–66.

Ur, P. (2012). *A course in English language teaching.* (pp. 91–94). Cambridge: Cambridge
University Press.

20 Draw attention to correct answers

In most cases, it doesn't naturally occur to us to comment on something correct in students' production. But it's a great learning opportunity.

This could be defined as providing error correction without the error: just drawing attention to correct or appropriate language!

In the 'Discipline' section there's a tip saying 'Compliment good behaviour'. This is the same sort of thing, but its purpose goes a good deal further than simply making the students feel good and reinforcing desired behaviours. Of course, when you draw attention to language that has been used correctly and appropriately by a student, that student will naturally be pleased. But it also has two further positive results.

The first is the learning of the item by the rest of the class. It's really nice to be able sometimes to use students' own written or spoken production as a source of new language, or as a basis for reinforcement or review, rather than your own speech or the texts from the coursebook. Students are likely to respond positively, and 'notice' the item well. And there's the feeling 'If he/she can do it, so can I!'

The second is that if students know you are going to comment on good things as well as mistakes, that's going to help motivate them to write more freely, and to speak with more confidence in front of the class.

Here's an example from my own, fairly recent, experience. In an EAP (English for Academic Purposes) course I teach in my college, participants give presentations on their research interests, supported by slides. As they're speaking, I note down positive aspects of their presentation (language, style, design of the slides, etc.) as well as mistakes or awkward expressions. And I refer to both in the following feedback session. It has become a popular routine, singled out in participants' feedback as a particularly useful feature of the lesson.

Games

Games that involve engaging with the language are useful for raising motivation, especially (though not only) for younger classes. But they need to be carefully selected or designed to make sure they do in fact work: that they are both 'gamey' and learning-rich.

---

21 Make sure games are fun

22 Check games are learning-rich

23 Keep games simple

24 Involve all, or most, students

25 Have more than one winner

---

21 Make sure games are fun

> Check that your game is in fact a game: something which involves some kind of fun challenge.

'Let's play a game,' said a teacher I once observed. 'I'll say a word, you write it down.' After a few such 'games', the students groaned whenever the teacher said 'Let's play a game', and the word lost its meaning.

The point about a game is that it has some kind of challenge that is fun to overcome. Sometimes this is simply competition with an opponent or opposing team; but more often in the classroom it is created by setting a task that is obviously easy, but whose achievement is limited by rules. For example: 'Find out what I have in my hand, **but** you can only ask 'yes/no' questions,' (a simple guessing game). Or: 'I'll give you all sorts of simple commands (e.g. 'Stand up!'), **but** you must only obey the command if I also say 'Please',' (my variation of the game 'Simon Says').

The problem with the teacher's so-called game above was that it was no fun. If she had said: 'I'll say six words straight off without pausing, see if you can remember and write down at least two of them,' then there's an element of challenge, and choice, and the activity becomes more game-like.

A lot of routine activities can be made into games by adding this element of challenge.

Let's consider for example the standard activity of practising vocabulary by making up a sentence that contextualizes it. As it stands this is pretty boring, but it gets to be more game-like if you add a condition: 'Make up a sentence but it must use **two** of the words on the board'; or '… but it must be a true statement about yourself'; or '… but it must be obviously untrue'. Or simply add a time limit: 'You have exactly two minutes: how much of the task can you do in that time?'

Check games are learning-rich

> It's important that the students are not only having fun playing the game, but also getting some benefit in terms of language learning. This isn't always obvious, so you need to check.

There are many games that keep students happily occupied, but the actual language-learning or review involved is, if you think about it, minimal, and playing them is probably a waste of lesson time. A lot of word games are like this: 'Wordsearch', 'Hangman', 'Word jumbles', 'Find short words from the letters of a long word like *INTERNATIONAL*'. If you analyse how the time is being used, you find that more than half of it is spent searching and puzzling, rather than finding and solving; and even when there is a solution, there is little or no engagement with the meaning or use of the word found. So I'd recommend using these only for short 'fillers', or for keeping a restless class occupied at the end of the day.

In contrast, guessing-games ('Guess what I'm miming', for example) involve students in using the language meaningfully and practising interrogative forms: they are creating and understanding questions and answers in English all the time the game is going on.

Another family of learning-rich games is those that invite playful responses to a cue. The challenge is for students to brainstorm as many imaginative, original or funny ideas as they can. For example:

- How many uses can you think of for a tin can?
- What do you think this 'doodle' represents?
- What has just happened to these people (shown in pictures)?
- How many different reasons can you think of for opening a window?

The winners are those individuals or groups who produce the most, or the most original, ideas in the opinion of the teacher. Alternatively, you can just play the game for the fun value of the contributions, with no specified winner.

Keep games simple

> Avoid games that have a lot of stages and take ages to explain, or need elaborate materials. Time taken to explain or distribute and collect materials is time taken away from the game itself.

It's best to use games that you can explain and demonstrate very quickly and then do, with minimal further organization of materials. Otherwise you may find that a lot of the time you have allotted for the game is spent explaining the different stages of the game and answering questions; or distributing and later collecting boards, cards, dice and so on.

An example is the game BINGO. Each student has a card divided into five-by-five squares, each square with a target picture or word in it. The teacher has a stack of cards similar to these squares. He/She selects one at random and calls out the word. A student who has it on his or her grid claims it and covers or marks it on his or her grid. The first one to complete a five-square line calls out 'Bingo' and is the winner.

Here's a simple alternative version which I learned from Andrew Wright. Write up 15–20 words on the board that you want to review, and ask each student to choose and write down five of them. Call them out (or give definitions or translations), and as the students identify their own words they cross them out. The first to cross all of them out calls 'Bingo'. It's the same game, the same fun value, similar type of practice – but so much easier and quicker to organize.

By the way, the same principle of 'keep it simple' applies to your own preparation. Try to avoid games for which you have to prepare lots of bits of paper or card; unless, of course, you're fairly sure you'll use them repeatedly in the future. In this case, it's worth laminating such cards or paper so they'll last longer, and saving a digital version on your computer.

Involve all, or most, students

> Try to make sure that your games have all, or most, of the students actively playing them, rather than single individuals.

Games that directly involve only one or two students while the rest look on not only lead to less learning, but also tend to be less interesting and fun for all concerned. An example is team games where one team representative comes to the board to perform a task and gain a point for their team, while everyone else is inactive. So try to adapt games so that most, or all, of the students are active for most, or all, of the time.

In the usual version of 'Simon says', for example, (see Tip 21), usually anyone who does the action when they shouldn't is 'out' and sits down. But to increase participation, tell students to keep playing, and continue until you feel they, or you, have had enough. Then they have to tell you how many times they got it wrong (never, once, twice, or more than twice).

A lot of full-class games, like guessing games for instance ('Guess what animal I'm thinking of') involve everyone, potentially, but only one at a time. So once students have got the idea through a full-class demonstration, let them play it again in small groups. More students will participate, and even if they lapse into mother tongue (L1) or make occasional mistakes, the quantity of practice of English, and the fun, will improve.

One more technique to improve the quantity of participation in any game which involves multiple contributions (guessing, or brainstorming lots of possible solutions) is to skip the procedure where students raise their hands and you nominate one to speak. Just let everyone call out their questions or ideas freely as they occur to them, and you respond to contributions as you catch them. Obviously you can't easily do this in big or rowdy classes: but when you can, many more students are active, and there is greater game momentum.

Have more than one winner

> In games that involve competition and there can be only one winner, some students will often be disappointed, and less likely to enjoy the game: particularly the younger and/or less advanced ones.

I don't use competitions in class very much, at least not those that result in one winner, for the reason given above. I prefer team games – when a whole team feels they won rather than a single student.

Alternatively, I tweak standard competitive games to ensure several winners. For example:

'Simon says': I play it in the way described in Tip 24, rather than continuing until only one player is left; and then proclaim that the winners are those who made a mistake never or only once.

'Bingo': I use the version described in Tip 23. The first person to call 'Bingo' is a winner; but then I keep calling out the words – and the last student (or students) to cross out their last item and call 'Bingo' are also winners. That way there are two or more winners. (Also, I am able to get through reviewing all, or most of, the items instead of having to stop as soon as one person has finished.)

Then there are competitions where students compete against themselves rather than against others. For example: 'Say things about a picture'. In groups, students are given exactly two minutes to say everything they can about a picture (one from their coursebooks, or one displayed on the board), while a secretary notes a tick ✓ for each sentence contributed. Then they count up ticks. The second time round, they do the same with another picture, with the goal of beating their previous record. Normally, everyone wins.

For more games see the reference below.

Wright, A., Betteridge, D., & Buckby, M. (2006). *Games for language learning* (3rd ed.). Cambridge: Cambridge University Press.

Grammar

I'm definitely in favour of teaching grammar in most classes. The problem is how to do it effectively so that it doesn't take up too much time, doesn't become boring, and helps students use the grammatical features to express themselves.

26 | Keep explanations short

> The first time you explain a grammatical feature, make it short and simple: keep it to a 'need to know' basis.

What students need is to get the basic idea of how the grammar works in order to enable them to understand examples in context as soon as possible, and try using it themselves.

Note that there's a payoff between brevity and truth: the more true and accurate the rule you give, the more difficult and lengthy the explanation. So often it's worth sacrificing the fully accurate account in favour of keeping it short and simple. Give students a clear, easy and mostly reliable rule and leave any further detailed explanations for when they come across apparent exceptions.

For example, most other languages have only one word for *much/many*, so you need to explain the difference between these. But you don't have to get into complicated explanations of 'countable' and 'uncountable' nouns. All you need to say is that *much* goes with singular nouns and *many* with plural, which covers virtually all instances.

Some rules are so complicated and difficult to apply in real time that it's best not even to try to explain them. For example, expression of future time: *going to* usually implies some kind of plan or intention whereas *will* expresses simple prediction. But who has time when talking about the future to stop and wonder how much planning is involved in any particular instance? So I usually tell beginner classes that both forms refer to the future, and leave it at that. Detailed explanations can wait for later: and often I've found I never need to give them, because the students acquire an intuitive feel for the distinction through lots of encounters with examples in context.

For more on this issue, see the reference below.

Swan, M. (2012). Design criteria for pedagogic language rules. In *Thinking about language teaching* (pp. 45–56). Oxford: Oxford University Press.

Use mother tongue to explain 27

> It's often helpful to students if you explain the grammar in their mother tongue (L1) – if you know it! – and also compare it with parallel mother-tongue usages.

With more advanced classes, of course, you can use English: an excellent opportunity for listening-comprehension practice.

But the language you need to explain a grammatical feature is often far more advanced than the feature itself, and can be very difficult for less proficient students. So it can take ages to explain in English a relatively simple point. Normally you can get the idea across in a fraction of the time if you use L1, and then use the time you've saved to let the students hear, read and try using the target grammar themselves.

It also helps students a lot if you contrast how the English grammar works with how a parallel structure works in their L1, particularly if the L1 does not use a structure that English does, or vice versa. Let's take the example of the verb *be*. Arabic and Hebrew don't have a present tense of this verb at all; Spanish, in contrast, has two verbs (*ser* and *estar*), where English only has one. It saves a lot of confusion and mistakes if you tell students about these differences at a fairly early stage. Similarly, where English and the L1 have different forms to express the same meaning, it's worth contrasting: for example, the French *elle est professeur* as contrasted with the English *she is a teacher*.

In principle, the fact that students have a mother tongue is an asset, not a hindrance. It is not something to be avoided, as you may have heard some people claim, but rather a tool to be exploited where – as in these examples – it can help students learn English better (see the reference below).

Hall, G., & Cook, G. (2012). Own language use in language teaching and learning. *Language Teaching*, 45(3), 271–308.

28 Avoid grammatical terms

> If you can explain a form or rule in English grammar
> without using grammatical terminology like *comparative
> adjectives, present perfect* and so on – do so.

When you are talking about grammar in English, some basic
grammatical terms that apply to a wide range of structures are useful to
teach: words like *form, meaning, word, sentence, past, present, future*.
And lot of these will be useful in general communication as well, not
just for grammar explanations. But the use of more specific terminology
may not be very helpful.

For one thing, an explanation which uses the actual exemplars rather
than the terms used to define them is likely to be easier to understand.
For example, say 'We use *the* when...' rather than 'We use the definite
article when ...'. Or: 'Use the *–ing* form of the verb after words like
enjoy...' rather than 'Use the gerund...'. When explaining to younger
classes when to use *a* and when *an* there is no need to use terms like
vowel/consonant; I usually show them that it's just uncomfortable to try
to say *a...orange* (demonstrating with a pronounced glottal stop), and
much more comfortable if you smooth the way by putting in the *n: an
orange*.

A second reason is that such terminology is not really very useful
vocabulary to learn. How often will the students need to use a term
like *past perfect* in real-life communication? It's simply not a good
investment: if you're going to teach new words, it makes sense to teach
more useful ones.

The general principle of using actual examples from the language rather
than the terms that refer to them applies to instructions for grammar
exercises as well. So in an exercise on relative pronouns, for example,
it's better to say 'Write *who, which* or *that*', rather than 'Write the
appropriate relative pronoun'.

Get students to learn by heart

> If students know a few samples of the use of a grammatical structure by heart, they can often create more of their own, intuitively feeling what is 'right'.

Knowing rules helps students learn to use grammar correctly; but so does learning examples by heart. Which is more effective depends both on the student's learning style and on the target feature being taught. It's probably a good idea to use both.

Learning by heart doesn't have to be boring rote-learning. Here are a few ways of doing it:

- Clichés, proverbs, etc. Teach the students common expressions that also exemplify grammatical features: useful and frequent phrases that occur in conversation, as well as clichés, idioms and proverbs. For example, *I don't know*; *Let's call it a day*; *All's well that ends well*.
- Chants. Learning and performing rhythmic chants – like songs, but without the music, and imitating the rhythm of natural speech – is great fun, and very helpful (see the first reference below).
- Songs. A lot of songs also feature repetitive grammatical phrases. The problem is that the melody distracts from the meaning, and students can often enjoy singing them without paying attention to the actual language features used.
- Dialogues. Having students learn and perform dialogues – preferably dramatic and thought-provoking ones – is an enjoyable and useful way to get them to learn grammar. They can then introduce different vocabulary, or add bits, to create varied meanings. (See Tip 74.)
- Pattern poems. When students create simple poems round a grammatical pattern, they inevitably learn and review the grammar as they write. A student who writes such a poem learns the lines by heart as a side-effect (see https://www.njcu.edu/cill/vol4/moulton-holmes.html, or the second reference below).

Graham, C. (1993). *Grammarchants*. Oxford: Oxford University Press.

Holmes, V. L., & Moulton, M. R. (2001). *Writing simple poems: Pattern poetry for language acquisition*. Cambridge: Cambridge University Press.

Get students to make meanings

In order to learn a grammatical feature, the students need practice in using it to make their own meanings. Conventional grammar exercises are not enough.

The problem with traditional grammar exercises (gap-fills, matching, etc.) is not only that they are a bit boring, but also, and mainly, that they focus too much on 'getting it right', and not enough on creating meanings. The fact that students can do a grammar exercise perfectly is no guarantee that they'll then be able to use the target feature in their own speech or writing. They need practice in expressing their own ideas with the grammar, not just manipulating sentences someone else has written. I'm not saying that the traditional exercises are useless – far from it! – only that they are insufficient on their own.

The trick is to think about what the grammar means and how it's likely to be used in real life. Then use this knowledge as the basis for some kind of cue or situation that would invite responses involving use of the target feature. For example: the present perfect is used when the action, state or event has already taken place, but has some relevance to the present. So give the students a present situation, as shown in a picture – for example, an untidy room – and ask them to say what has happened to produce it, or what has not yet happened. Or if you've been studying modals like *can, should, might* – invite students to say what they *can/should/might* do in a particular situation; or what a particular type of person (a teacher, the President of the United States, a baby) *can/should/might* do.

These can easily be made into brainstorming games (see Tip 22).

See the reference below for further similar ideas.

Ur, P. (2009). *Grammar practice activities* (2nd Ed.). Cambridge: Cambridge University Press.

Group Work

Group work is very useful for some purposes, such as getting students to talk, but some teachers tend to avoid it because of concerns that it may result in an uncontrolled process with little learning going on. In order for group work to go smoothly and work as it should, it needs to be carefully designed and planned.

31 Have a good reason to use group work
32 Make collaborating worthwhile
33 Do group work in the middle of the lesson
34 Use pair work a lot
35 Instruct before making groups
36 Organize groups quickly
37 Arrange endings in advance

31 Have a good reason to use group work

> It's good to have students collaborate in order to learn but only if this does in fact lead to useful learning. Group work is not necessarily a good thing in itself.

The importance of using group work has, in my opinion, been rather over-rated in the professional literature. Here are some things to think about before you decide whether or not to divide the class into small groups for specific tasks:

- In some lessons I've observed, group work involves only 'busy work' or 'sharing of ignorance', with little learning. You need to make sure there is some substantial language learning or practice going on.
- Sometimes group activities can be difficult to control in classes where students are easily distracted and tend to go off-task.
- Some tasks are inappropriate for group work and are better done individually (see Tip 32).
- Students vary a lot in the way they like to learn. Although some enjoy working in groups, others prefer to do things on their own, or in teacher-led full-class activity, and dislike collaborative work.
- Classes may have different previous experiences of group work. If they've done a lot of it in the past, or regularly use it in other subjects, then it's easier for you to use it in your own lessons. But if they haven't, you may encounter reluctance or even opposition.

So by all means use group work occasionally, but you don't have to feel guilty if you don't do it very often! Use it when you're sure, and can make clear to the students, that working in groups will achieve aims that you couldn't achieve so effectively through individual or full-class activity. For example, I normally use group or pair work for oral fluency tasks, because there's no way all the students can have opportunities to practise talking in a full-class discussion (see Tip 73).

Make collaborating worthwhile 32

Not all tasks are appropriate for group work. If a task can be more conveniently done by an individual, then there is unlikely to be much collaboration even if it is done in groups.

An example of this is: 'Work together to compose a paragraph about…'. Writing is essentially an individual activity. If there is one student who is good at writing and has plenty of ideas, then he or she will inevitably do most of the work, even if the group has been told to collaborate.

Tasks that are more appropriate for group work are those where it's obvious that a better result can be obtained by collaboration than by any one student on his or her own, however proficient that student may be.

Brainstorming activities, for example, based on pooling original ideas, will clearly get more responses and better results if done in groups: 'How many uses can you find for a pencil, other than writing or drawing?' Or 'Sally has no money to buy a birthday present for her mother: how many suggestions can you make as to what she might do?' Or even simply: 'How many words can you think of that have to do with [a given theme]?'

Recall activities are, similarly, better done in groups: 'How many of the words we've learnt over the last two weeks can you remember?' 'Close your books and recall as many as you can of the items in the exercise we've just done.'

Another possibility, which takes a bit more preparation, is to design the task so that each student has only one bit of the information or material necessary to achieve the goal. For example: a group of five students get a set of twenty words, four words for each student. They have to make up a story together using all the words: a sentence including one of 'their' words is contributed by each participant until all the words have been used up.

33 Do group work in the middle of the lesson

It's a good idea to have your group work planned for some time in the middle of the lesson: not to go straight into it at the beginning, or have it carrying on right to the end.

In general, group work tends to be a more lively, 'stir'-type activity (one where the interaction is lively), whereas the beginnings and endings of lessons need to be more 'settling' (quieter and more restrained). (See the article referred to below.)

More specifically, the beginning of the lesson is best used in general for teacher-led work on new language or texts (see Tip 4): it's when students are at their freshest and most receptive. But when you've spent time on focused work on new material, it's good to move into a different mode, to step aside and let the students work with each other rather than being directly led by you. The end of the lesson, on the other hand, should normally consist of a full-class rounding-off activity (see Tip 2). Letting group work run right to the end of the lesson doesn't allow for this.

Another reason for timing group work for the middle of the lesson is that it's quite difficult to predict exactly how much time it will take. Even after a lot of experience, I'm never quite sure how long a particular group task will take with a given class. Planning it for the middle of the lesson allows you the necessary flexibility. If it takes more time than you'd expected then you've left yourself the possibility of spending longer on it, even if it means abandoning something else you'd planned. If, on the other hand, the process comes to an end sooner than you'd expected, then you are able to stop it earlier, and add another reserve activity.

Maclennan S. 1987. Integrating lesson planning and class management. *ELT Journal* 41(3): 193–197.

In many cases, pair work gets better results than group work: it's easier to set up and control, and ensures more participation.

Getting in and out of groups can be time-consuming (see Tip 36), but pairs are much easier to organize: just get students to turn to face the person next to them (or in front of or behind them). And for some reason I've found pair work a lot easier to control than groups of three or more: perhaps because the closeness of the partners to each other means fewer distractions, and there is no need for regulating turn-taking.

The main advantage of pair work, however, is the amount of active participation. At any one time at least half the members of the class are active; there's virtually no possibility of one student remaining passive and letting others dominate.

Most of the activities you can do in small groups you can do also in pairs; and there are a lot of fun tasks that are particularly suited for pair work. For example:

- Picture dictation. One student tells the other what to draw. Or there's one basic drawing: the students take it in turns to tell each other what to add, change or colour. (If all the pairs have started with the same basic picture, they later display the different results.)
- Reverse guessing. Each student has a pile of words, pictures, or situation-descriptions. He or she provides hints or descriptions until the partner guesses the answers.
- Information gaps. Each student has a table or form partially filled in; the missing information in one student's table is shown in that of his or her partner. They ask and answer questions in order to fill in all the missing information.
- Things in common. Students talk to each other in order to find out at least three (non-obvious) things they have in common.

35 Instruct before making groups

It's important to ensure that students know what they are going to do before they actually move into groups.

Putting students into groups can be quite a challenging process (see Tip 36). So sometimes you feel that you need to complete the organization into groups first, and then give instructions, which seems more straightforward. This is a mistake! And one that I made lots of times before I learnt the hard way that it's better to do it the other way round.

If the students are in groups or pairs, they are naturally facing each other, and their attention is therefore directed within the group, not towards you. But you need the students' undivided attention for your instructions. They should be facing you, with full eye-contact, in order to ensure that they listen to you and understand exactly what they will be doing once they are on their own.

There are various other things you can do to make sure the instructions are clear before they start:

- With less advanced classes, give the instructions in their mother tongue (if you know it).
- Write up the instructions on the board as you give them.
- If you've given the instructions in English, ask one of the students to repeat them in their mother tongue (if this is understood by all participants).
- Do a demonstration or rehearsal of a sample task with a volunteer group of students while the rest watch.

Finally, give students the opportunity to ask questions if they feel anything is unclear; and get a 'yes' to the question 'Do you all understand what to do?'.

Then, and only then, divide students into groups and tell them to go ahead.

Similarly, don't give out any task materials before groups have been formed. The materials will draw students' attention and some of them may not listen to your instructions on what to do with them. Display sample materials, if necessary, before the class and refer to them as you instruct.

> A lot of class time can be wasted getting students into groups. So you need strategies to help you achieve this quickly and smoothly.

It's usually not a good idea to ask students to form groups on their own. This is not only very time-consuming, but also tends to result in unbalanced group compositions, often with the more advanced students getting together and the less proficient left to form other groups. Also, you may get groups of widely varying sizes which you then have to even out; and sometimes less popular students may find themselves left out. So it's usually best for you to take the initiative in deciding who will work with whom.

There are various strategies used by teachers to divide classes into groups. These two are my favourites:

- If they are sitting in rows, tell each pair of students in a row to turn to face the pair behind them – and so on. This saves moving around and is probably the quickest way to form groups.
- Number off all the students in the class, according to the number of groups you want. So if you want five groups, number them off 'One … two … three … four … five … one … two … three …'. Then all the ones get together, all the twos and so on.

Sometimes – though very rarely in my experience – there is the problem of students who refuse to work together. Once you know your class, you will find ways to make sure you avoid putting them together, or move them quickly if your strategy has put them in the same group.

In general, once groups have been formed that work together well, I keep them fixed for a few weeks or more before changing them. If students know their groups then they move in and out of them very quickly and smoothly.

37 Arrange endings in advance

Sometimes it's difficult to draw group work to a close. It helps a lot to build in arrangements for ending within your initial instructions.

Make sure from the beginning that the students know what the signal to stop will be. It could be simply that you call out 'Stop!'; it could be a bell or buzzer. Some teachers tell the students that they should stop talking when he/she raises a hand. (This one has never worked for me, but some of my colleagues have used it successfully.)

It's also very useful to give a time limit in advance: 'We'll draw the activity to a close at eleven o'clock / after ten minutes'. If students know time has run out, it's much easier to stop them; and you can always add extra time if needed, or finish early if you see the activity has come to a natural end. A useful additional tip here is to give advance notice two minutes, say, before the time limit is up: 'You have two more minutes, start finishing'. (Incidentally giving a couple of minutes' advance notice that an activity is going to end is a good idea not just for group work, but for any procedure not directly teacher-led: for example, individual work, extensive reading, or computer work.)

Although some tasks can go on indefinitely, others (decision-making, for example) clearly end when the goal of the task has been achieved. With these, some groups will inevitably finish earlier than others. So prepare a reserve activity in advance to keep them occupied. This could be an extension of the original task (such as writing a summary of their decisions), or a new one, or just going back to their places in the classroom and getting on with reading or homework. But in any case, make sure that students know in advance what they will be asked to do if they finish early.

Heterogeneous (mixed-level) classes

A well-known half-joking definition of a heterogeneous class is 'a class of two': as soon as you have more than one student, you have heterogeneity. You always need to cope with different people among any student group. So these tips are applicable to virtually all classes.

Let students choose

> Whenever you can, allow students some choice in the items
> they want to answer in a language exercise, so they can opt
> for those that are closer to their level or interests.

Textbooks don't usually allow for student choice in exercises. They
usually just give directions like *Match* ... or *Complete* .... You can
introduce an element of choice by using one of the following strategies:

- Start where you like. Read through (without answering) a set
  of question items, then tell students they can raise their hands
  to answer any of the items they like. So one student who wants
  to respond to a more challenging item that happens to be
  question 7, or another who wants to answer an easier one that
  is question 10 – can do so immediately. The same can be done if
  the students are writing down their answers.
- Do any six of the questions. (Or five, or three, or whatever.)
  This works best for written work. The principle is the same
  as the above. Make sure the exercise is understood by all the
  class, and then tell them to choose which questions they want to
  answer and which they don't.
- Work cards. (My favourite, I must have done this one hundreds
  of times.) Compose or adapt from a textbook or website ten or
  fifteen brief 'bite-sized' tasks each of which will take only short
  time to do. Put each on a card or separate slip of paper; you'll
  probably need two or three copies of each. Put these at a central
  point in the classroom, perhaps on your desk. Each student
  chooses a slip, writes his or her responses in a notebook, and
  then brings it back and chooses another. Make sure students
  know they aren't allowed to write on the original slips! If you
  think you'll use the slips again, then paste them onto card and
  laminate them.

Attend to the weaker students

> It's normally the stronger and more confident students who are the more active participants in the classroom process, and therefore tend to be the ones that get attended to by the teacher.

It's also, to be honest, easier and more enjoyable to deal with students who get it right and can express themselves fluently and with fewer mistakes. It's much less comfortable to interact with those who misunderstand, are hesitant, who constantly make errors. And yet these are the ones who need us most, and for whom our teaching can make more of a difference.

So the bottom line is that in a heterogeneous class we need to try, as far as we can, to give most of our attention to students who are under-achieving.

It's quite difficult to do this in a full-class interaction, where the more advanced students quickly raise their hands in response to your questions, or even shout out answers. So first of all do insist that students wait to be nominated before answering (unless you're deliberately using a rapid brainstorm interaction like that suggested at the end of Tip 24). And it's a good idea to allow quite a lot of wait-time before eliciting answers, to give slower students more of a chance to make a contribution. Try telling students that you won't choose anyone to answer until you see at least ten hands raised. Then when choosing who is to answer, prioritize those who volunteer less often.

In individual work, it's easier. While the students are working on individual reading or writing tasks (perhaps allowing for some choice, as suggested in Tips 38 and 40), find time to sit by those who find it more difficult, and offer help and support. This can, of course, be done in small groups: gather three or four of such students together in a corner of the classroom, and work with them privately for a few minutes.

40 Invite different answers

It's important to use mostly open-ended questions or cues in heterogeneous classes: ones that allow for a variety of answers.

Closed-ended questions – those that have only one right answer – are by their very nature homogeneous. They are designed for one level of learner. Students below that level will find them too difficult and either not do them at all or get them wrong. Those who are above the level will answer them easily but won't benefit much and will quickly get bored.

It's fairly easy to make closed-ended items into open-ended ones. To practise modals, for example, you might have a closed-ended item like *Jenny is a baby, Jenny _____ ride a bicycle* with the options *can/can't*: the answer is obviously *can't*. But if you then say 'Jenny can't ride a bicycle, tell me some other things she can or can't do' – then the exercise invites all sorts of answers based on *can/can't* at different levels. A less advanced student might say 'She can't walk' or 'She can smile'; a more advanced one might say 'She can crawl' or 'She can't open a bank account'. Make sure that there's a possibility of making very simple responses, for the less advanced students. The more advanced ones will always find more complex ones.

Another advantage of such items is that they lend themselves to personalization. When I do the exercise described above, for example, students have told me later that they found themselves basing their answers on a particular baby they know (a baby sister, for example).

One of the problems with so-called 'interactive' computer-based language exercises, incidentally, is that they are nearly always closed-ended (so that the computer can tell you if you're right or wrong). They provide useful drilling, but aren't very suitable for a heterogeneous group of students.

(For more ideas how to transform closed-ended into open-ended exercises, see Tip 9.)

Limit tasks by time, not amount

> Learning tasks are normally defined by quantity: 'Do six
> questions, finish reading the text, write a paragraph' and
> so on. But for a heterogeneous class it's better to define by
> time: 'Do as much as you can in ten minutes'.

Students differ a lot in the speed at which they work. What takes one
student an hour to do, another might be able to finish in twenty minutes
or less. Ideally, each student should be allowed to work at his or her
own pace, and a slow-working student should not be made to feel bad
because he or she has not done as much as the others. So it makes sense
to define the achievement of the goal of an activity by time not amount:
'Your task is to work for ten minutes and do as much as you can'. A
task defined in this way can clearly be successfully completed by all
members of the class, regardless of level.

With students who are responsible and autonomous learners, this
strategy can also be used for homework: 'Read your books for half an
hour; do as much as you can of the exercises on this website in twenty
minutes'.

The use of a time limit has other advantages. For one thing, it helps
with transitions. If the students have been working on their own on a
reading or writing task in the classroom, you can more easily stop it
when the given time is up, avoiding (or at least lessening) protests from
students who want to carry on and finish. For another, it's a nice way to
introduce a game-like challenge, and adds motivation. Instead of saying:
'Work in pairs and do these questions', try saying: 'Work in pairs on
these questions. You have exactly five minutes: let's see how many you
can do!' (see Tip 25).

42 Give basic tasks plus options

> Tell the students: 'Everyone has to do task A', (where task A is obviously doable by all the class); 'Task B is optional for those who finish A'.

The aim of this strategy, as with that of giving a time limit (see Tip 41) is to fix the success-level of a task as one that is clearly achievable by all, regardless of individual proficiency or speed of work. So anyone who finished Task A has succeeded in doing the assignment; anyone who also does Task B has succeeded even more. The choice is, as it were, between success and more success rather than between success and failure.

Most coursebook tasks can be presented this way, with a slight change of wording in the instructions. Say something like: 'Do at least … and if you have time do …'. The basic 'at least' task could be the first few questions of an exercise; or reading the first paragraph of a reading passage; or writing four lines of a story. Alternatively, give a complete – but relatively easy – exercise for the first task, and another, more challenging, one for the optional extra.

Some students do need a bit of a nudge from the teacher to make sure that they do, in fact, go for the optional extra if they are capable of it! Others need reassurance that it's OK just to do the basic one.

I also use this strategy for written tests. Most of the sections of the test are compulsory, and of a level I am fairly sure most or all the class can manage with a bit of an effort. Completing these perfectly would get the student a grade of 100%. But then there's an extra, optional, question which may be slightly more demanding, but also more creative, which can only be done by students who have completed the compulsory sections. Doing this question earns 'bonus' points. (For more details on this, see Tip 86.)

Homework

The students can't learn all the material they need to only through classroom interaction: the supplement they get from doing regular home assignments is essential. Homework tends to be a neglected topic in many teacher-preparation courses, but well worth some attention.

43 | Clarify requirements in advance

> Devote a few minutes at the beginning of the course to explaining to your students how much homework they'll be regularly asked to do, how often, and so on.

Students like to know in advance what the homework requirements are going to be. Sometimes, of course, norms may be determined by the institution: for example, that homework is usually given three times a week, or even that it is not given at all. It's a good idea to check also with colleagues to find out how they do it in different classes. And I suggest in addition finding out students' ideas on the subject: you don't have to do exactly what they want, but it's useful to be aware of their preferences.

Some things which the class should know from the beginning about homework are:

- How often it will be given.
- Whether it should be submitted on paper or digitally (and if digitally, using what software).
- How long you will normally expect them to spend on a homework assignment.
- How, and how often, homework will be checked.
- Whether homework assignments form a part of their final grade for the course (see Tip 45).
- How punctual they are expected to be with submitting assignments, and what happens if they are late.

It saves a lot of misunderstandings and arguments later if such things are clear from the start, and observed consistently throughout the course.

Sometimes it happens that you find a rule you laid out at the beginning of the course about homework – or, indeed, about anything else – isn't working very well in practice. In one of my own classes, for example, I said I wouldn't accept late assignments, and then found that I was too soft-hearted to implement my own decision! In such cases you need to publicly change the rule – or your own behaviour – otherwise students are likely to relate to other decisions of yours as equally unreliable.

Make homework success-oriented 44

> A homework assignment is done without any teacher
> support, so it needs to be something which students know
> they can do successfully on their own.

Homework assignments should be in principle slightly easier than ongoing classwork. It should be clear to students when they receive them that they are able to complete them successfully on their own at home. Make sure the tasks won't take too long to do, or involve a lot of vocabulary they don't know yet. So it's not usually a good idea, for example, to ask students to read difficult or long texts at home.

Besides selecting a reasonably easy task to do for homework, here are some other things you can do to help students succeed:

- Do a similar task in class. So then all you need to say is 'Do Exercise B, which is the same sort of thing as we've just done together'. Students will then be familiar with the format and process of the assignment, and confident they know how to do it.
- Ask students to re-do for homework the same exercise you've done in class: a reading text with comprehension questions, or a grammar exercise, for example. This may sound boring; but actually it usually isn't, because it's done fairly quickly and easily, and includes a bit of a challenge to memory: they need to recall answers, as well as understand the material.
- Do the first section, or first few items, of the assignment together with the students in class. Their homework is then simply to complete it.
- Allow students a few minutes in class to start doing the assignment while you are available to answer questions or give help; they finish it at home.

P.S. A major problem, in general, with homework is that a lot of students simply don't do it! So this and some of the other tips in this section are designed to help ensure that they do (see also Tips 45, 47 and 49).

45 Include homework in the final grade

If there is a final grade for the course given by you, it's a good idea to include homework-doing as one component of it. The fact that they know they will get credit for homework in their grade is, for many students, an added incentive to do it regularly.

For many students it is vitally important to pass the course with a good grade. This may make all the difference to their continued studies or job opportunities. They therefore will invest particular effort in tasks that clearly contribute to this grade: tests, for example. If neglecting to do homework does not directly affect the grade, such students may see it as optional, and not bother to invest much effort in doing it. Conversely, they will do their best to complete all the homework assignments if it is made clear from the beginning that this will add points to their final assessment.

Apart from that, surely it is only fair that students should get credit for conscientious completion of homework, not just for doing tests well.

If you accept this idea in principle, then you need to decide how much of the grade will be allotted to homework: 15%, for example.

Then there is the question of whether students will get credit for assignments done particularly well, or whether it's enough just to complete them all. In principle, of course, it would be good to give extra points for well-done homework, but most of us don't have time to check and grade every assignment of every student (see Tip 49). My own solution is to keep a record of whether students have or have not done assignments with a simple ✓ opposite their name. When I do check an assignment in detail, I note a ✓✓ for any done particularly well, an ✘ for any done badly, and take these into account when allotting the final grade.

Prepare homework-giving in advance 46

> It's not enough just to note down in advance what homework you are going to assign; you need to think about how you're going to give it, and at what point in the lesson.

I've suggested elsewhere (see Tip 5) that it's not normally a good idea to give homework at the end of the lesson. The main reason is that this often doesn't give you time to explain it properly and answer questions. Too often I've seen homework given as a sort of afterthought, when students know it's the end of the lesson, are packing up, and don't really pay attention to what the teacher is saying.

You need to plan, and allow several minutes of lesson time, for the following:

- Giving clear instructions. It may be necessary, in beginner classes, to give these in the students' mother tongue, if you know it, in order to be quite certain that they understand. Another useful strategy is to perform a sample of the 'kind of thing' you are asking them to do with volunteer students, in order to clarify. For example, do one or two of the items of the exercise, or write a elicit a sentence or two of a written assignment.
- Writing up the homework on the board as well as just giving oral instructions. Doing this makes the assignment clearer, and also enables you to come back at the end of the lesson and remind students about it, pointing to the note on the board.
- Giving students the opportunity to ask questions, in order to clarify anything that isn't clear to them.
- Telling them **why** you are giving it. It's important for students to be aware what the learning purpose is: that it's not just given arbitrarily for the sake of giving homework!
- Getting students to write down the assignment in their notebooks, including the date when it is due.
- Optionally, giving them time to start doing it in class (see Tip 44).

47 Check homework has been done

> Responding quickly to students' homework conveys the message that you care that they do it, and raises motivation. And vice versa.

I was recently talking to a student who said that she'd stopped doing homework simply because the teacher gave it but then paid no attention to whether it had been done or not. In an ideal world, of course, we'd like students to be autonomous, to understand the value of homework, and to do it for the sake of the benefit to their own learning. But in most situations it doesn't work like that: they need your attention to, and appreciation of, any assignments they have done out of class.

Note that there's a difference between your feedback on **whether** the homework has been done at all, and **how** it has been done. It's an important distinction, but sometimes teachers confuse the two. Of course you do need to check how well homework has been done: but not all assignments, and not every time (see Tip 49). But it **is** essential to check every time whether each student has made a reasonable attempt at it. Here are some ways you can do this:

- Simply ask them: and note by a list of their names who says they have done the homework and who has not. On the whole, I find that I can trust them to tell the truth; if there's a doubt, you can always check.
- As students are checking answers collaboratively or individually, (see Tip 48), walk round the classroom and note who has and has not done the homework.
- Ask students to lay their notebooks open at the page at which they did their homework; walk round the class checking while they are doing individual work or reading.
- Ask them to send you the homework by email or through a website. Again, note who has or has not done it.

Keep class checking to a minimum   48

> We can't usually take in and correct all our students' assignments personally, and checking homework publicly in class seems like a good solution. But don't do this too often: it can be a serious waste of lesson time.

I've observed many teachers starting the lesson by checking homework through a 'ping-pong' interaction. A student volunteers an answer to a question, and the teacher approves or corrects it while the rest of the class listens. Then on to another student and the next question. This can take up to half the lesson. It's often a waste of time, because the students have already done the assignment, and the repetition can be boring and contribute little to learning. Feedback on homework is much more effective if we take in individual assignments and give personal responses (see Tip 49). Lesson time is better spent teaching new material, or reviewing, or managing communicative tasks.

I'm not saying never check homework in class. Sometimes you simply don't have the time to go through the individual assignments at home, and this is the only alternative. However, do it as little as you can and when you do, try to avoid using the time-consuming 'ping-pong' interaction described above. Here are some other possibilities:

- Dictate the answers: students self-check.
- Write up the answers on the board: again, students self-check.
- Ask students to work in pairs or small groups checking and correcting each other; they ask you only if there's something they aren't sure about.
- Finally, if you know everyone has done the homework (see Tip 47), and you are sure that most or all of them have done it well, compliment them, and don't do any detailed checking at all.

The exception to all this is when your goal is not simply checking, but rather additional learning: when you feel it's important to go through the homework exercise again thoroughly, or re-do it another way (see Tip 10).

49 **Check written homework**

If you have a lot of large classes and a heavy teaching load, it may not be possible to check and correct every written assignment; but do as much, and as often, as you can.

There are two stages to feedback on a written assignment: the first is the checking, by you, that the homework has in fact been done (see Tip 47); the second is more detailed, personal feedback on the content.

Sometimes assignments can be checked in class; but this can take up a lot of valuable lesson time (see Tip 48). And it's important in principle to provide regular personal written feedback. This is partly because if students have invested effort in doing homework, it is only fair to respond to this with effort of your own by providing feedback; and partly because students will benefit more from such feedback if it is personal. Ideally, every assignment should be given in, corrected, commented on and returned within a day or two. This can be done if you have relatively small classes and not too heavy a teaching load. For many of us however, this is not feasible: there are simply too many students, too many homework assignments, and not enough time.

Here are some possible solutions:

- Take in only a third, say, of the students' assignments each time to check in detail, and make sure that over time you do get to see assignments by every student.
- Take in all the assignments, but check only part of what they have written: only five of ten questions, for example, or only one paragraph of a written assignment.
- Give homework in the form of an online exercise, which automatically corrects and provides a grade. You can then check the online records, note results, and let students know when you have done so.

Whatever you decide to do (you may have another idea I hadn't thought of), make sure students know about it in advance (see Tip 43).

Interest

Time and work invested in making the lesson interesting is well worth the effort. A class of students interested in the tasks you give will try harder, learn better, and is likely to be easier and more pleasant to work with.

50 Don't worry about the topic

> A good topic helps, of course, to arouse interest, but it's not as vital as you might think. It's all too easy to kill a fascinating topic, and to bring to life an apparently uninteresting one: it's the task that matters.

It's quite difficult to give a recipe for a good topic. In general, topics that are relevant to students' lives, or culture, or personal experience are likely to be interesting (see Tip 54); but sometimes ones that engage students' fantasies or imaginations, totally removed from their own reality, can be just as good. Your best guide here is your own knowledge of your students, and your intuitive 'feel' for what they will relate to with interest.

But in any case, even after you've found a topic that is interesting to most of the members of the class, this will help to engage them only at the beginning of the activity or text. Interest will be maintained only if the treatment of the subject is interesting as well. If the topic is, for example, 'football' – when you know most of the class play it and eagerly support the local team – then this is likely to raise students' motivation to participate. However, if the content of the text is merely a description of the rules of football, or if the activity consists of learning vocabulary items connected to the game, then students are likely to lose interest. A topic such as 'numbers', in contrast, looks boring: but if you ask each student to write down a number that is personally significant to them, and then share it with their classmates, they'll continue to be motivated to say and understand numbers in spite of the apparently uninteresting nature of the subject (see also Tip 99).

So by all means look for topics that interest your class, but remember that the important thing is not what they are, but what you do with them.

Keep activities short and varied

> A lesson – unless it is very short – should normally be broken up into different activities. The use of short, varied activities prevents students getting bored, and helps them to concentrate.

This is particularly true of younger and less motivated students; but it applies in principle to any class. I have an EAP class whose members, a small group of highly motivated academic researchers, have told me that they find it difficult to concentrate during long (60–90 minute-) sessions all focusing on one task, and appreciate the fact that the session is planned to include varied components.

Normally, in a lesson of 45–60 minutes try to do at least three different things; though of course you may want to do four or five in some classes, maybe only two in others. If you've been spending time on a difficult reading text, perhaps go on to a game practising oral fluency. If you've been doing a lot of teacher-led work, then move to group or pair work. Alternatively, if you feel it important to get through a long text in one lesson, for example, perhaps take a break in the middle to do a brief activity for a few minutes, to give your students a 'breather' (see the reference at the bottom of Tip 12 for some ideas).

Keep in mind that there are a number of different ways you can vary activities. You can change:

- the skill; reading, writing, listening or speaking, or a combination;
- the focus; communication or accuracy-oriented language work;
- the level of difficulty or challenge; whether a task requires effort or is relatively easy;
- the speed; whether the activity involves rapid interaction or slower, reflective work;
- the classroom organization; teacher-led, group/pair or individual;
- the materials; textbook, paper, the board, computers, or hand-held devices;
- movement; whether the task involves moving around or sitting still.

52 Tell students what the goals are

> It makes a huge difference to students' interest in doing
> something if they know why they are being asked to do it.

Any learning activity has in fact two major goals:

1   The 'surface' goal of the task. For example, a grammar exercise may
    have the goal of completing sentences correctly. A discussion task
    may aim at reaching a consensus on the solution to a problem. A
    listening comprehension task may require students to fill in a table
    according to information the students hear.
2   The underlying language-learning goal. The grammar exercise, for
    example, is intended to improve students' awareness of, or ability to
    use, a particular grammar feature, and perhaps to avoid a common
    error. The discussion task is done in order to improve oral fluency
    and discussion skills like turn-taking. The listening comprehension is
    intended to improve students' ability to understand a listening text,
    or perhaps a specific accent.

Sometimes there may be other goals that are worth drawing students'
attention to. For example, a particular activity may replicate a
component of an exam the students are going to take, and is therefore
a good preparation for it. Or you may have a social goal: getting to
know one another, or increasing class solidarity. In other cases, you may
design an activity as a way of familiarizing students with a digital tool
or some new software that you intend to use in future lessons.

You will naturally tell students what the surface goal is, but remember
that even if they seem obvious the underlying goals are also worth
making explicit. Sharing with students the rationale for what they are
doing shows respect for them and raises them to the status of aware
cooperators in the learning process, rather than obedient pupils. And
they will be more interested in doing something whose aim they
understand than something arbitrarily dictated by textbook or teacher.

Doing something through the use of higher-order thinking skills – such as distinguishing differences or similarities, prioritizing, generalizing, classifying, problem-solving or creating new ideas – is much more interesting than using lower-order thinking skills such as identifying or recalling single items.

There are of course a lot of good educational reasons why we should be incorporating higher-order thinking skills, including analytical, critical and creative thinking, into our teaching, and there's plenty of literature on how to teach them. (Have a look at the online slide show referred to below.) But a major reason that is relevant particularly to language learning is their contribution to interest.

For example, when practising vocabulary it is common to ask students to complete sentences with a word that needs to be practised; or to match words to their definitions or to pictures; or to identify the nearest synonym in a multiple-choice question. All these exercises are based on pretty boring, lower-order thinking processes. But if you ask students to classify a set of abstract concepts such as 'beauty', 'formality', 'controversy', 'peace', 'war', 'strength', 'rejection' as 'positive', 'negative' or 'neutral' – you get deeper thinking, and the activity is much more interesting. Another example: instead of the conventional 'odd one out' exercise with one obvious exception (e.g. *elephant, horse, dog, fish, sheep*), provide a set of items where there is no obvious exception (e.g. *elephant, horse, dog, sheep, monkey)*, and invite students to think up reasons to justify each in turn as the 'odd one out'.

Very often the use of open-ended cues (those that have lots of right answers) will stimulate higher-order thinking skills, particularly creative and original thinking, and result in more interesting and sometimes amusing responses. (See Tip 9 for some ideas for how to transform conventional 'one right answer' exercises into open-ended ones.)

Wooi, T. (2016). Teaching higher order thinking and 21st century skills. Available from http: www.slideshare.net/timothywooi/teaching-higher-order-thinking

54 Personalize

> It's usually more interesting and easier to talk about things that are personally relevant than about things detached from students' own lives.

Textbooks these days are much more likely than they used to be to invite students to talk about their own experiences or opinions. But still, there's a limit to how much they can do so, since the textbook authors don't know the students. You, however, do, and are in a position to 'personalize' a lot of the tasks. Writing and speaking tasks are fairly easy to personalize: for example, you can ask students to write about their own experiences ('Write about a time when you were disappointed / amazed / delighted'), or give them discussion tasks to exchange information about each other ('Find out five things you didn't know before about your partner'). In work on listening and reading, you can ask students for their own responses ('What would you have done ...?' 'What do you think of ...?') to complement the standard comprehension questions.

A lot of grammar exercises use names of fictional characters as subjects or objects of the sentences. For example: *Sheila doesn't need ... help (no/any/some)*. Try asking students to substitute the name of someone they know, or someone else in the class. It's a very simple change, but immediately brings the exercise to life.

When working on vocabulary, instead of telling students to work on the sentences in the book, or to compose ones to contextualize the target items, ask them to make up ones that are true for them, and include the word *I* or *me* as well as the target vocabulary item. Or invite them to relate an item to someone they know; or a place they know; or a familiar situation.

It's very easy to tweak language exercises in this way, and demands no preparation. It just needs a bit of thought and awareness of the need to personalize whenever you can.

Use visual materials 55

> Visual materials attract attention and interest; and the more colourful and appealing they are, the better.

For most people, it is sight which is the dominant sense: so much so, that if you don't give your students a visual focus that will keep their attention, they will search for another, which may distract them.

You yourself are probably the most important visual focus in your classroom. So be aware that you are 'on show', and use facial expression, gesture and movement to make what you are saying more interesting.

The second most important one is the board, whether a conventional white- or blackboard, or one with a digital display. Use it not only for writing but also for drawing. Don't worry if the pictures are funny – most of us are not very good artists! It doesn't matter, as long as they are just about recognisable.

Reading and writing are, of course, by their very nature based on visual material. It's best if reading texts are also illustrated, or use colour or varied fonts and headings that make them more interesting to look at; but this is not usually under your control. Use written or graphic materials also as a basis for oral fluency work. Students will find it far easier to think of things to say if they have something relevant to look at, or if the task itself is based on a visual stimulus. (See, for example, the one mentioned at the end of Tip 25.)

The main problem is listening, because a lot of the listening exercises in textbooks or online require students to listen to recording without seeing anything – and it's very difficult to maintain interest in a voice without seeing the speaker (see Tip 59). If you can, use video or a live speaker as the source of the listening text, or provide a relevant visual stimulus such as a picture or simple text that is relevant to the content.

Listening

Listening is probably the most important of the four skills: it's the starting point for learning any living language, and most people spend more time listening – including listening during conversation – than they do speaking, reading or writing.

56 Give topic and task in advance
57 Don't always pre-teach vocabulary
58 Don't use written texts
59 Let students see the speaker
60 Divide the text into short bits
61 Use dictations

Give topic and task in advance   56

In classroom listening exercises, it's important to tell students in advance about the topic and context of the text, and to give a task, so that they are prepared for what they are going to hear, and know what they have to listen out for.

Just asking students to 'listen and understand' is a bad idea. It's quite frustrating and uncomfortable to try to understand something without any previous idea of its context and what it's going to be about. The listener has to try to work out who is talking and in what situation, as well as trying to grasp the meanings, with no advance clue. This is a complex set of tasks which we almost never face in real life. Think of any situation where you had to listen and understand recently: in most cases you'll have known in advance who would be talking, what the situation was and the sort of things you were likely to hear. Even in a phone conversation, the speakers normally identify themselves and the caller says why they are calling before starting the conversation. So on both counts – making understanding easier for the student, and preparation for real-life listening situations – it makes sense to provide this information before students start listening.

Similarly, we normally have a purpose in understanding what the speaker is saying (again, think of a listening situation you've encountered recently). In the classroom, this purpose is supplied by the listening task. So don't tell students to listen and then afterwards face them with comprehension questions: give the comprehension task in advance. If it's questions, then give students time to read these before listening (and sometimes it's a nice idea to encourage them to guess what the answers are going to be – they can always correct themselves later). There are a number of other kinds of comprehension tasks that can also be given in advance: *Make notes on …*, *Find out …*, *Fill in as much as you can of the table … .*

57 Don't always pre-teach vocabulary

It's surprisingly unhelpful to pre-teach vocabulary before giving a listening comprehension task.

Teachers are often told to pre-teach vocabulary before engaging with a written or spoken text. Though this may be useful in giving students some idea of what the text is about, it doesn't actually help comprehension very much. The problem is that being taught a new item once does not enable a learner to identify and understand it readily when they encounter it afterwards in a new context. Normally, several re-encounters are necessary to reach this kind of ability (see Tip 92). So if you know students are going to need a certain set of vocabulary items for a listening text, teach them well in advance and leave yourself time to review them a few times before the listening task. Or teach only one or two vital items, so that the load on memory is less and there's more chance that they will be recalled. Or – preferably – simply use easier texts that you know the students can manage to understand pretty well without needing new vocabulary at all.

There's some empirical research to support all this. Chang & Read (see the reference below) tried four types of strategies to help with listening comprehension: repetition of the text itself, pre-teaching of vocabulary, advance reading of comprehension questions, and providing information about the content. Of all of these, the pre-teaching of vocabulary helped least, and providing information about the topic helped most (see Tip 56).

This doesn't mean that you should never pre-teach vocabulary. Teaching new items, then hearing them used in a text, then re-encountering them in comprehension work and further review exercises can contribute to eventual real mastery of the vocabulary. All I'm saying is that pre-teaching the vocabulary in itself before listening doesn't help comprehension of the listening text very much.

Chang, A. C., & Read, J. (2006). The effects of listening support on the listening performance of EFL learners. *TESOL Quarterly*, 40(2), 375–397.

Don't use written texts

The kind of listening text that results from a written text being read aloud is both unnatural and relatively difficult to understand. Try to use texts that replicate natural conversation as far as possible.

Textbook listening texts and online podcasts used for comprehension work often consist of a written text read aloud. It's easy to see why. Authentic conversation is tricky to record, and often very difficult to understand, being full of overlaps and indistinct utterances. It's much easier to read aloud and record a prepared written text.

But written discourse is meant to be read (normally silently), not heard. It's far more densely packed with information than natural speech, lacks the redundancy, pauses, and repetitions that make spoken conversational English easier to understand for a listener, and uses more difficult vocabulary. So it's a lot harder to follow when read aloud. Have you ever had to listen to lecturers who just read aloud their papers from a prepared written text? They are far more difficult to listen to and understand than those who deliver their content by talking directly to the audience.

Most of the spoken discourse that our students will need to understand in real life, moreover, will be improvised, informal conversational English, and that's what they need practice in listening to and understanding. Learning how to understand written text read aloud will be of limited value.

The problems with recording natural conversation remain. Some possible solutions are to use:

- your own improvised speech: for example, giving students information in your own words or improvising your own version of a story, perhaps based on pictures;
- discourse that was composed to imitate natural speech, while ensuring comprehensibility: for example, screenplays of films, or scripts of plays;
- recorded talks or monologues by professional lecturers or actors.

For more on this point, see the reference below.

Ur, P. (1984). *Teaching listening comprehension*. Cambridge: Cambridge University Press.

Let students see the speaker

> Try not to use audio-based listening comprehension
> activities too often where students are listening 'blind' to
> spoken text. It's so much easier (and more natural) if they
> can see the speaker.

The reason why audio recordings usually provide the basis for listening
comprehension tasks is – like the use of written text read aloud –
basically a matter of convenience. They are much cheaper and easier to
produce than are video recordings. But there isn't much real justification
for their use, either in terms of good classroom activity design or in
terms of preparation for real-life listening.

Good classroom activities should be interesting and not too difficult to
succeed in doing, as well as providing plenty of engagement with the
target language feature. Activities based on audio recordings arguably
provide plenty to listen to, so fulfil the last condition. But they are much
less interesting to do because they lack the visual element (see Tip 55).
And they are less likely to be successful simply because it is so much
more difficult to understand spoken discourse when you can't see the
person producing it. The speaker's facial expressions, lip movements
and body language all contribute to understanding.

In real life, moreover, we usually see the person we're listening to. There
are exceptions, like when you're listening to the radio or talking on
the telephone. But think back over the last day or two when you were
listening and understanding speech in your mother tongue. How much
of it was spoken by an invisible speaker? Probably very little.

There is, certainly, a place for practising listening to things like
telephone messages or radio news but most listening comprehension
should, for the reasons given above, be based on speech coming from
either live speakers (yourself, or a visitor, perhaps) or speakers shown
on video clips, television programmes or films.

Divide the text into short bits 60

> Try not to have your students listen to long stretches of unbroken discourse, like a five-minute talk for example, and then respond. It's not very useful, quite difficult, and can get tedious.

In natural listening situations the discourse we listen to is normally broken up into fairly short fragments. The most common such situation, of course, is ongoing conversation, when what we hear is normally interspersed with our own contributions. But many other kinds of listening situations are also characterized by short bursts of speech, punctuated by pauses, changes of speaker, different visual focuses and so on. Some examples are a scene from a movie, an interview, a talk accompanied by slides, a television commercial, loudspeaker announcements.

It's not only more natural, it's also much easier to concentrate if we can listen to short rather than long stretches of discourse, particularly if these are in another language. So even if your basic text does consist essentially of one long speech – a lecture, for example, or a story – try to find ways to break it up: pause the audio or video recording occasionally, or stop to invite student responses.

Asking students to respond as the listening is going on has other advantages. I've already mentioned the problems with giving comprehension questions after the students have finished listening (see Tip 56). It's much more natural and useful to have them respond as they listen. They can't, of course, simply say their answers out loud – the most natural response – because of the constraints of the classroom situation. But they can write brief notes, check off lists or insert ticks or crosses by true/false statements.

P.S. The only situation when you can allow yourself longer stretches of speech and don't really need any explicit ongoing response at all is when you are telling a good story. The students' expressions and body language provide all the evidence of comprehension that you need!

61 Use dictations

> Dictations are not just a test of spelling. When they are based on full utterances rather than single words they are a surprisingly good way to practise listening comprehension at elementary levels.

Dictation is the activity of having students write down text read aloud by the teacher. It's useful at the beginning stages when students are learning the sounds and writing system of the language. It's often mistakenly thought to test or practise only spelling, with the aspect of listening for meaning largely ignored.

But dictation gets students to listen as well as write, and is not so meaningless an exercise as it seems. I'm learning Spanish at the moment, and find that I am totally incapable of writing down a Spanish sentence correctly from dictation unless I understand it. Try having someone dictate a sentence to you in a language you don't understand, and see how far you get! In other words, dictation, when based on complete phrases or sentences rather than single words, requires listening comprehension, and can be used to practise it. And there is some evidence that it does so quite effectively. A group of Iranian learners who also did regular dictations scored significantly better on listening tests than others who had only done routine listening tasks (see the reference below).

In order for dictation to function as listening practice, say short utterances or sentences at a slightly slower pace than normal, but retaining the flow of natural speech, and repeating two or three times. Tell students not to worry too much about the spelling. If they clearly understand the text – have made correct word divisions, and only trivial spelling mistakes – then treat their answers as right. (Though you might give them 'bonus' points for correct spelling!)

Reza Kiany, G. & Shiramiry, E. (2002). The effect of frequent dictation on the listening comprehension ability of elementary EFL learners. *TESL Canada Journal*, 20(1), 57–63.

Pronunciation

The goal of pronunciation teaching is to get your students to speak with an accent that is easily comprehensible to listeners who are themselves speakers of other mother tongues: it's not usually to get them to speak with one of the 'native' accents.

62　Teach pronunciation (a little)

> Of all the aspects of language – vocabulary, grammar, pronunciation, spelling, the four skills and so on – pronunciation is probably the one that needs least teaching.

I never used to teach pronunciation at all, because in the place where I worked pronunciation was not treated as an explicit teaching goal, and there were no pronunciation explanations or exercises in the Ministry-approved textbooks. Later, when I learned about teaching situations elsewhere, I discovered that this was unusual: in most places pronunciation does get some attention. But it appears (though I have no research evidence to support this) to be less emphasized than it used to be. This is probably due to the changing context of English teaching. The goal of speaking English like a native speaker has been largely replaced by the aim of being able to communicate in a variety of situations worldwide, usually in interaction with other people whose mother tongue is not English. So we want our students to speak using pronunciation that is widely and easily understood, not necessarily one that is a replica of one of the native English accents. A mother-tongue accent is perfectly acceptable, provided that it is not so strong as to make difficulties for the listener (see Tip 63).

If this is accepted as the aim, then in many cases students can learn to pronounce English fairly satisfactorily without much explicit instruction, though this depends, of course, on how difficult the pronunciation of English sounds is for your students . The primary model for students' pronunciation is teacher talk (see my tips on this later in this book); but there's also television, movies, the internet, popular songs, and so on.

Having said this, however, some learners encounter specific problems which can be helped by occasional focused teaching. The other tips in this section make a few suggestions. See also the book referred to below.

Hewings, M. (2004). *Pronunciation practice activities: A resource book for teaching English pronunciation*. Cambridge: Cambridge University Press.

Drill isolated sounds

> Not all language use in the classroom has to be meaningful! It's useful sometimes to isolate and practise problematic sounds.

I remember the first time I went to France to do an advanced course in French, wanting mainly to improve my speaking skills. My speech wasn't very fluent and my accent not as good as I thought it was. I don't naturally have a very good 'ear' for pronunciation, and it really helped me when the instructor isolated a sound I was consistently getting wrong (the [y] as in *rue*) explained what I was doing wrong, contrasted my pronunciation with the correct sound and made me practise until I got it right.

Most of us can identify particular sounds that our students tend consistently to mispronounce. For example, the unvoiced aspirated English /p/ sound is very difficult for many Arabic speakers, who tend to substitute a voiced, unaspirated equivalent that sounds like /b/. In such cases, conscious, focused drilling is a good investment. Once students have had their attention drawn to the new sound and have spent time and effort practising getting it right, it's likely to stay a permanent feature of their pronunciation.

This is, of course, rather time-consuming, so you can't drill all the sounds students get wrong – there are so many other things to teach, and pronunciation is not usually a top priority! (See Tip 62.) You need to decide which items are important to get right. One obvious criterion for selection is communicative meaning. Ask yourself which sounds if mispronounced are likely to lead to misunderstanding. There's some very revealing research on this (see the reference below). Another criterion is what I would call 'listener comfort'. If a certain mistake in pronunciation is resulting in speech that it is uncomfortable for another person to listen to, even if they can understand it, then this is also a reason to provide guidance and focused practice.

Jenkins, J. (2002). A sociolinguistically-based empirically researched pronunciation syllabus for English as an International Language. *Applied Linguistics*, 23(1), 83–103.

64 Contrast with mother-tongue sounds

> Many mistakes in pronunciation arise because the learners are pronouncing the English sound similarly to how they'd say a parallel sound in their mother tongue. It can be helpful to show the learner how this is happening and how they can overcome it.

Clearly when a Spanish speaker pronounces *school* as *eschool*, or a German speaker says *vot* instead of *what*, this is because in Spanish consonant clusters like /sk/ are always preceded by a vowel, and German doesn't use the /w/ sound, but pronounces the letter w like an English 'v'. These are the kinds of mistakes that can indeed sometimes affect comprehension and 'listener comfort' (see Tip 64). Students can be made aware of such points through various means:

- your own explanation, based on your experience of learner difficulties and your knowledge of the students' mother tongue;
- handbooks on teaching pronunciation: see particularly Appendix 2 in the book referred to at the bottom of Tip 62, which lists pronunciation difficulties encountered by speakers of various languages;
- *YouTube* clips which raise awareness of the differences by explaining to an English speaker how to speak English with a foreign accent (try searching for "speak with a French accent", for example).

One fun way of making students engage with such issues is by asking them to say their own names in an exaggerated English accent. If they can't yet do this, then do it yourself and ask them to imitate you. Then discuss what the differences were between this pronunciation and the normal mother-tongue one. A variation is to do this the other way round: provide English names, ask students how they would pronounce them in their mother tongue, and again, raise awareness of the differences through discussion. Or contrast the pronunciation of 'international' words that are used, with slight variations, in a number of languages: *radio, telephone, football, jeans, pasta, microphone*.

Having identified some problematic differences, the English sounds can be practised as suggested in Tip 63.

Teach 'international' pronunciation

> A lot of teachers worry about whether to teach British
> or American pronunciation. I'd suggest teaching
> the pronunciation of any word in the way which is
> internationally most acceptable, even if the overall result is
> a mixture of British and American.

If you are a native English speaker, or have been taught a particular
variety of the language, then that is the pronunciation you will naturally
teach. However, many students today are exposed through television,
movies and the Internet to a variety of accents, and you'll find them
coming to you and asking which is the 'right' way to pronounce
something. For example, in my own classroom I naturally pronounced
the word *girl* without the /r/. But my students often heard it with the /r/
sounded, and were confused as to which version should be their model:
I remember one student telling me she thought I pronounced it wrong!

Most students are learning English not in order to interact with native
speakers but with people who themselves are speaking English as an
additional language. So the criterion for 'good' pronunciation, is not
'How near is it to a specific native-speaker accent?' but rather 'How
easily will it be understood by most English speakers today?'.

I would, therefore, encourage my students to pronounce the /r/ in
girl for two main reasons. First, because that's how it's pronounced
in a standard American accent, which on the whole predominates
in international discourse (as do standard American vocabulary and
spelling). Second, because it's nearer to the spelling. Most people
learning English as an additional language are learning both the spoken
and the written varieties: and it helps comprehension a lot if the written
and spoken form correspond. This doesn't always favour the American
version. For example, a word like *hostile* is pronounced much closer to
the spelling in a British accent.

So teaching international pronunciation can result in a mixed American
and British accent, plus mother-tongue influences. Which is fine.

Reading Comprehension

The reading text is normally the first and most important component of a textbook unit and the basis for later language work. So it's worth investing some thought into how to make it accessible and learning-rich.

Read aloud while students follow   66

It can be very difficult for students to try to cope with a new text on their own. It's made a lot easier if the teacher reads aloud while they read along.

The reading text, which is normally a prominent feature of any course unit, is usually studied intensively and 'milked' for vocabulary and grammar. But because a lot of this language is new, the texts are likely to be relatively difficult for the students. We need, therefore, to think about how to support their understanding of the content. Pre-teaching some of the vocabulary can help to some extent, though possibly not as much as we might expect (see Tip 57). But perhaps the most learner-friendly and effective way of mediating a new text is to read it aloud while students follow. There's some research to confirm this (see the reference below).

When you read the text, you intuitively use appropriate prosody: group the words into sense-patterns, insert pauses in the right places, and add appropriate intonation. This is what clarifies meaning. In addition, it's easy to stop every now and again to explain new words as you feel necessary. And you can keep an eye on your students, pick up any expressions of incomprehension and respond as necessary.

But you do have to make sure that they are in fact following the text! I find that when I read aloud some of them tend to raise their eyes, look at me, and abandon the reading completely. The exercise becomes a kind of listening comprehension – which defeats the purpose! You need to keep glancing at your students, make sure they are reading, and move to help ones who have lost their place.

Amer, A A. (1997). The effect of the teacher's reading aloud on the reading comprehension of EFL students. *ELT Journal*, 51(4), 43–47.

67　Minimize guessing from context

> Guessing from context is a reading strategy encouraged
> by many methodologists; but actually it's surprisingly
> unreliable as a way of accessing word meaning.

In one research study on *inferencing* (guessing from context) strategies
used by intermediate students in reading new texts, it was found that
they inferenced correctly fewer than 50% of the unknown words
(Nassaji, 2003). This is confirmed by informal checks I've run with
teachers. Even when the text is in your mother tongue, you normally
cannot accurately infer the meaning of a new word from context and
need to look it up in a dictionary.

If the aim is just to get on with understanding the content of the text
rather than learning new language, then inferencing is, of course, useful.
When students are reading their own graded readers, for example,
or going through an informational text to get the main ideas, then
it's probably enough to inference the rough meaning of unknown
words. Or they may just skip them altogether and get the overall idea
without them. But if a major aim is learning new vocabulary – as it
usually is when studying a coursebook text – inferencing is simply not
reliable enough, and may be frustrating and time-wasting. It's probably
best simply to give the meaning of the word yourself, or provide an
explanation or translation in the margin.

One reason you might nevertheless sometimes invite students to guess
from context is in order to help them develop inferencing skills to use
in their own reading. So you might ask them 'What sort of thing do you
think this word means?' – get some suggestions, and then move swiftly
on to provide the correct meaning. But don't spend too much time on it.

Nassaji, H. (2003). L2 vocabulary learning from context: Strategies, knowledge sources
and their relationship with success in L2 lexical inferencing. *TESOL Quarterly*, 37(4),
645–670.

Don't make students read aloud   68

> **If a student is reading aloud a new text, his or her attention is necessarily on pronunciation and phrasing, not on comprehension.**

In some classes, students are used to reading aloud a new text and may request to do so; this has happened to me occasionally. But when I agree, I've often found that the students who have just read a sentence aloud cannot immediately tell me what it was about. They had been concentrating on decoding and pronunciation, and had no attention to spare for understanding meanings.

It's useful to hear students reading aloud at the early stages of learning, to make sure they are pronouncing letters or letter combinations appropriately. But later we should mostly focus on silent reading, which allows the full attention of the reader to be directed towards understanding, and is eventually much faster than reading aloud.

Many students do *vocalize* at the early stages – murmur the words to themselves, or just mouth them silently – as they read. But that's not as demanding as public reading. And you don't need to discourage it, if students feel it helps. They usually grow out of it naturally as they learn to read faster and find that vocalizing slows them down.

Reading aloud in English, moreover, is not in itself a very useful skill for most students' future lives, and therefore not something it is important to give practice in. It's essential for teachers, of course, or professional newsreaders. But even these people don't normally sight-read; there is usually some possibility of preparation and rehearsal.

So on all these counts, try to avoid asking students to read aloud text they encounter for the first time. However, if it's a text they are already familiar with and understand, reading aloud may be useful (see Tip 70).

69 Read and re-read

> The simple act of re-reading a text improves comprehension, even without any further instruction or explanation on the part of the teacher; and even more so if there is some teaching input.

Re-reading of a text provided in the coursebook as the basis for a unit is important for various reasons. First, as stated above, the re-reading itself improves comprehension. I often find myself going back to re-read a passage that at first encounter I didn't understand, and find it gets clearer second time round. Second, if the teacher has meanwhile taught some new vocabulary the re-reading enables students to re-encounter it in context and reinforce the learning. Third, it contributes to reading fluency. Students are able on second and third readings to get through the text, with understanding, a lot more successfully and faster than they could at the beginning.

The problem is, of course, that simply re-reading the text in the same way as you did at the beginning can get boring. You need to find different ways to do it. Here are some suggestions:

- Give students time in class to re-read the text silently. They ask you for help if there's anything they still don't understand.
- Give students some extra, more challenging questions to try to answer as they re-read.
- Tell students to re-read the text on their own at home using a dictionary if they find any words whose meaning they don't remember.
- If there is an audio recording of the text available, have students listen to it as they re-read.
- Call out a phrase or sentence, and challenge students to scan through the text to find it.
- Call out a phrase or sentence in the students' mother tongue and challenge them to find it in English.
- Give different students different bits of the text to prepare either at home or in class. Then have students read the texts aloud. (Note that this is quite different from the unprepared sight-reading described in Tip 68.)

Use readers' theatre   70

> In *readers' theatre*, students prepare and perform texts they have studied, distributing parts and rehearsing delivery, but without needing to learn the text by heart.

Readers' theatre is a technique developed in the United States, and used widely, particularly in China. Try searching on the Internet for the combination "readers theater" (using the American spelling). Most of the online video clips you will find show examples involving younger classes, but I have used it successfully with older ones, including adults. It is particularly appropriate for dialogue, poetry or narrative, but can in principle be used with most kinds of text.

Divide the students into groups and tell them they have to plan and will later perform an artistic reading of the text, or a specified part of it, designed to make maximum impact on the audience. So they need to think about how they will distribute the text, when they'll be speaking singly or in chorus, appropriate use of pause, intonation, volume, speed. They also need to consider what facial expressions, movements and gestures they will use. They are allowed to repeat bits of the text. In some cases – particularly with younger classes – you may invite them to use costume, sound effects and props: but these are optional, and involve more out-of-class preparation.

Even if exactly the same text is given to each group, I am constantly amazed by how differently the interpretations come out!

Readers' theatre is, in fact, another way of getting students to re-read the text (see Tip 69); but its benefits go further. It focuses the students' attention on meanings, and increases reading fluency. A side benefit is increase in vocabulary and spoken fluency. In many cases, the students get so familiar with the text through rehearsal that they actually learn some, or even all, of it by heart, and will be able later to use bits of it meaningfully in their own output.

71 Vary comprehension tasks

In many coursebooks, reading tasks are routinely followed by comprehension questions; but answers to comprehension questions may not always show comprehension (!), and tend to be a bit boring. There are other options.

Suppose you have a sentence in your text as follows: *The mostikurs were pangling the bauntries*. And then a following comprehension question: *Who were pangling the bauntries?*. You can easily give a correct answer (*the mostikurs*), but this does not indicate that you knew what the sentence meant. Unfortunately, a lot of comprehension questions are like this: they are too close to the original text and can be done successfully without full comprehension.

Even if they do check understanding, comprehension questions may be rather boring to do. Here are some other tasks you can use, without too much further preparation. You might ask students to:

- summarize the content of the text in their mother tongue;
- summarize the content of the text in English;
- think of an alternative title for the text, and justify it;
- in pairs, devise their own comprehension questions, exchange them with other pairs and answer;
- list ten key words or phrases in the text that they think are most essential for understanding the content;
- say which they think is the most important sentence in the text, and why;
- re-write the text in simple English for a less proficient learner;
- re-write the text in a different style (more formal/more informal);
- re-write the text as a different type of text (e.g. an email, an interview);
- write some questions they'd like to ask the author;
- write a criticism or review of the text;
- re-write the text relating it to a person, topic or situation they are familiar with.

For more ideas, see Maley, A. (1995). *Short and sweet*. London: Penguin English.

Speaking Activities

A lot of students are very unwilling to speak English in the classroom because they're shy, or worried about making mistakes, or afraid of losing face. So many either don't speak at all or use mother tongue instead of English. We need to think of ways to make it easier for them to participate.

Use language practice for fluency

> Often you can use standard grammar or vocabulary
> exercises as a basis for getting shy or lower-level learners
> to speak English.

Even the most mechanical grammar exercises, if done orally in the
classroom, can give students basic speaking practice. Get students to say
full-sentence answers out loud once and then when you've approved or
corrected, tell them to repeat the sentence more quickly and smoothly
without looking at their books.

Grammar or vocabulary activities that have more than one answer (are
'open-ended') and require creative oral responses will naturally give
basic practice in speaking, as students are saying 'their own thing', even
if this is grounded in a given sentence pattern. For example, if you are
practising the comparative form of adjectives, give students a basic
sentence like: 'A car is faster than a bicycle', then ask them to think of
other ways of comparing a car with a bicycle. They might say 'A car is
more comfortable than a bicycle' or 'A bicycle is cheaper than a car' and
so on. You have given your students a basic pattern so have made things
easier for them to construct their sentences – but they are choosing their
own adjectives, and the nature of the task ensures that they must create
meaningful sentences. (Theoretically, they could come up with nonsense
sentences like 'A car is wiser than a bicycle', but this has never happened
in my experience.)

If you use less structured cues, then of course students' responses are
more creative. For example, if you want students to practise the word
disappointed, you might ask them to tell you about a time they were
disappointed. Or if you want to practise the present perfect, you could
invite them to tell you about things they have never done and would
like to do.

(See Tip 9 for some ideas how to transform closed-ended language
exercises into open-ended creative ones.)

Dividing students into groups or pairs immediately multiplies the amount of time each student has to practise speaking. A class of 20 divided into five groups of four gives each student five times as many opportunities to speak as he or she would have had in a full-class interaction.

Of course, it doesn't work quite as simply as that! Inevitably there are some students who speak more and others less, in groups as well as in the full class. And groups that are not under your immediate supervision may lapse into their mother tongue some of the time, or do something that is not relevant to the task you have given.

But still, it's usually worth it. Let's take the example of a class of 20 divided into five. Even if half the time the students are speaking their mother tongue or doing something other than the task in hand, they are still getting more than twice as much speaking practice on average as they would have done in the full class.

There are other good reasons to use group work for oral fluency. First, it's much less scary to speak to a partner or a few other classmates in a small group than it is to say something in front of the whole class, so shyer students are more likely to participate. Second, the very fact that the people you are speaking to are close at hand helps: it's more natural to talk to someone nearby rather than to a whole group some of whom may be several metres away from you. Third, dividing the class into groups frees the teacher to walk around, monitor and help: to make sure groups are keeping to English, to encourage the less confident students to participate, even to make suggestions what they might say next.

(For some ideas on organizing group work, see Tips 33, 35, 36, 37.)

74   Let students use memorized text

> Using chunks of language learnt by heart is an excellent basis for oral fluency practice at the early stages of learning – and later as well.

First, there are dialogues. We can start off with simple, common fixed exchanges like – *How are you? – Fine, thank you*, and then go on to ones which can be the basis for variations: – *What's that? – It's a ….* And then start using brief, preferably dramatic or humorous, dialogues that can be performed in pairs or small groups: – *Where are you going? – I'm going away from here. – But why? – Because I've had enough.* (For some more ideas, see the reference below.) Students learn these by heart, perform them fluently, and the utterances are then readily available when they need to use them in their own later output.

The way dialogues are performed can be varied to add interest and fun. For example, you might ask students to do them fast, slowly, happily, sadly, angrily, loudly, softly. Or to replace or add words. For example: – *Where are you going? – I'm going away – to Canada.* And/Or they can do the dialogue imagining varied situations or characters: a mother and her son; a married couple; a pair of employees in a factory.

Second, it's useful to get students to learn by heart simple expressions that can be used in oral interactions: *Can you repeat?, I don't understand, No problem! Excuse me, I'd like to … .* Sometimes these can be enjoyably learnt within a sequence produced as a rhythmic chant (see Tip 29). And it's a good idea to display the expressions on the classroom wall as you teach them, removing each one as it is learned. More advanced students can also benefit from learning longer sequences that they can use in speech: common proverbs, for example (*All's well that ends well*), or idioms (*Let's call it a day*).

Ur, P. (2015) *Discussions and more* (p. 37). Cambridge: Cambridge University Press.

Give tasks rather than topics 75

If you tell a class 'Talk about X', you'll often find that students run out of things to say fairly soon. If you tell them 'Produce Y' – where they can only produce Y through talking – they are more likely to continue the discussion.

I've already discussed the importance of task as contrasted with topic (see Tip 50) with regard to maintaining interest in general, but the issue is particularly relevant to oral fluency activities. Some topic-centred discussions, like formal debates for example which are based on controversial motions like 'Speech is more important than writing', can work well, particularly in more advanced classes. But for elementary and intermediate classes who need less demanding and perhaps more specific ideas to get them to talk, a task is likely to work better.

A task, in this context, can be defined as something the students are asked to do that has a clear outcome – one that can be said, written down or drawn. A topic-centred discussion has no clear outcome, other than the exchange of opinions. (The final vote in a debate is secondary to the debating process itself.) But a task-centred discussion is goal-oriented. For example:

- Find ten differences between two pictures.
- Decide in what order of priority you would put a given set of qualities.
- Plan a party.
- Find as many uses as you can for a pencil.
- Decide which of five candidates you would select to win a prize.

(See the book referred to at the bottom of Tip 74.)

A good task is simple to describe and straightforward to do. For this reason, I don't usually use 'jigsaw' activities (ones which involve groups scattering and re-grouping in order to exchange and pool information), or ones that have too many stages.

If the task is done in groups (see Tip 73), then it's good to bring students together at the end for a full-class feedback session to hear and compare results.

Make sure the language is easy

> One of the things that stops students from participating in
> a speaking activity is that they simply don't have enough
> English to be able to say what they need to. So the task
> needs to be designed to use mainly language they already
> know.

If students feel they do not know the language needed to participate in
an activity, then they may not take part at all, or are very likely to fall
back on their mother tongue. This is another advantage of planning a
speaking activity round a task (see Tip 75): it's much easier to limit the
kind of language needed in a specified task, often based on a text or
picture, than in an open topic-based discussion.

For example, if you base an activity on a guessing game, then the
students will use a limited range of interrogative expressions like *Is it
(a) ...?, Do you ...?, Can we ...?*. If the activity uses a written text – for
example, choosing from a set of descriptions of potential candidates,
or deciding on an order of priority of a set of items – then the text
itself provides a lot of the vocabulary that the students will need to use.
Similarly, if it's based on a picture – as, for example in activities that
require students to say all they can about a picture, or find differences
between two slightly different ones – then the vocabulary is limited to
the items that are shown in the picture.

It's useful to review in advance words or expressions students are likely
to need for the task: the question forms they'll need for guessing, the
items that appear in the pictures, the language of the texts they are
discussing. Write up the key items on the board, so that students can
glance at them to refresh their memories as they talk.

Teacher Talk

In many situations teacher talk is the only source of spoken English the students have, so it's pretty important. But there's no point talking a lot of English if the students don't understand most of it. It becomes just a flood of incomprehensible noise, and all they learn is that English is incomprehensible! Teacher talk has to be clear and adapted to students' level.

77 Talk a lot

Contrary to some opinions you might have heard, lots of teacher talk in English is actually a good thing. It's an excellent source of English language comprehensible input.

The idea of the *learner-centred classroom* does not mean that students should be talking most of the time and the teacher keeping quiet, acting only as a facilitator. Of course, you want your students to be active language users for much of the lesson time; but you also want to give them opportunities to hear lots of comprehensible English, and learn from it. And the best such opportunities are provided by your own speech. It's likely to be better than recorded or filmed input, because it's directly addressed to your students, you can design and adapt it to suit their levels and needs, and it's 'live', taking place in real time.

Your spoken input is particularly important if your students hear little or no English outside your classroom – which is true for most teaching situations in the world today. In such cases, you are the only source of good spoken English your students will have. Listening to each other is not a substitute for listening to you. They need to have opportunities to listen to and understand input that is slightly more difficult and a lot more fluent than that which they can produce themselves.

Teacher talk can take the form of explicit language teaching: explanations of grammar or vocabulary, for example. Or it can be instructions on how to do an activity or what the homework is. Or feedback on student activity: corrections, comments on how something went, a summary of a discussion. Or initiatives of your own to let them hear you talk: stories (see Tip 79), or short presentations or talks (on the importance of learning English, for example!).

So don't feel guilty that you're talking too much, or that your classroom is too teacher-centred!

Keep eye contact   78

While you are talking to students, keep eye contact with them, or with as many of them as possible.

Speakers who talk 'at' their audience are not so well received as those who talk directly 'to' them: and the difference is primarily in eye contact. Eye contact both draws students' attention and makes it much more likely that they understand what you say. And if we are constantly looking at our students, we can more easily check their responses to what we are saying through their expressions and body language; we can pick up lack of comprehension, for example, and insert explanations or simplifications.

So don't gaze into the distance, and do keep your eyes scanning the entire class. Be careful you don't address only the students at the front of the class! And check that you don't have a preference for one side of the room, left or right. (Most of us do, unless and until we are aware of it and do something about it!)

Eye contact is a problem, of course, when you are reading aloud from a text. In this case, read slowly enough so that you can raise your eyes frequently from the page in order to look at the students. Or improvise your own version of the written text, adapting to the level of your students. And when writing on the board, take a break occasionally to turn round and glance at the students.

If you're standing at the front of the class, some students may be rather far away, and the eye contact less effective: so feel free to walk around, even speaking sometimes from the side of the class, or from the back. This not only adds variation, it also allows students sitting further back to see and hear you closer up, which helps attention and understanding and enables you to relate more immediately and personally to different members of the class as you speak.

> One excellent way of exposing students to spoken English through teacher talk is storytelling – not only for young learners.

When I'm in the middle of giving a talk to teachers, I sometimes digress from the explanations to add an anecdote that illustrates a point. I've noticed that the moment I indicate I'm going to tell a story, the audience perks up and becomes more attentive. There's a magic about stories that attracts attention and interest from listeners of all ages.

With younger learners, you can simply recount well-known folk tales or fairy stories. It doesn't matter that they've heard them before. On the contrary, children are happy to listen again to familiar stories (any of you who are parents will have experienced this first-hand!). And the fact that they already know them will make the English version easier to understand.

If you're using a picture-book, prepare beforehand – make sure you know the story – and then improvise the text yourself rather than reading aloud, showing them the pictures as you go. This is partly because the language of published stories intended for native speakers is often too difficult for the students, and using your own words enables you to simplify or occasionally translate. But it's also because improvising the text yourself enables you to talk directly to your audience and maintain eye contact (see Tip 78).

A variation on this, if you have a computer and screen available in your classroom, is to take an online video version of a story, turn down the sound, and tell the story yourself according to the events depicted on the screen. You can always pause the action if you want to explain or add further narrative.

For older students, anecdotes from your own life, as well as jokes, urban myths, strange events – easily found on the internet – are enjoyable to listen to and likely to keep students' attention.

> In order to enable you to keep to English as much as possible in your own talk, it's important in beginner classes to teach early on the kinds of things you will often need to say.

In general, the vocabulary we want to teach our students will be those items which are most common and useful in general communication, as shown in corpus-based frequency lists. An exception is classroom language. It's really useful for students to know common utterances of yours they need to understand for common interactions during the lesson, even if these will not be used very much once they leave the classroom. The following are ones I find helpful:

- Common instructions – usually prefaced with *Please*, like: *Sit down, Listen ..., Read ..., Write ..., Say ..., Open your books, Take out your notebooks / pencils / paper, Turn to page x, Talk to your partner, Get into groups, Be quiet, Wait a minute*;
- Common checks or questions: *Are you ready?, Do you have a problem?, What's the problem?, Do you understand?, Any questions?*;
- Common feedback phrases: *Excellent, Very good, Well done! Great! That's right, Can you say that again/another way?, It's better to say ... .*

In early lessons, deliberately teach one of two of these every lesson, review them later, and make sure you use them consistently thereafter.

All this does not, of course, ensure that the students will also respond in English (though it's useful to teach them stock phrases like *Please say that again* or *I don't understand ...*, so that they can, at least some of the time). The main point is that teaching students to understand this kind of interactive language enables you to use more lesson time on speaking English than you otherwise could; and by frequent exposure the students will be enabled in time to use the phrases themselves.

81 | Use mother tongue occasionally

> In most English teaching situations, students share a mother tongue (L1) which is known also to the teacher. There are still some teachers and teacher educators who claim that the L1 should never be used in the English classroom: but I don't agree.

Although obviously we want to maximize the amount of English that students hear during the lesson – as I've stressed in, for example, Tips 77 and 80 – this does not necessarily mean that we should never use the L1. If we insist on speaking exclusively in English when students are not understanding, we are conveying the messages that English is incomprehensible, or that it's OK not to understand – messages which surely we don't want our students to get. And a lot of students get frustrated and demoralised by their lack of comprehension: it makes them feel stupid.

A more positive argument is that the fact that students already know one language can be used to help learning. Occasional use of the L1 in our own speech can add clarity, provide useful insights into how the language works, and save time which can then be used for further engagement with English. So use L1 in, for example, the following situations:

- If there's an explanation of grammar or vocabulary which would be too difficult for the students in English, explain quickly in the L1 and then use the time saved to provide, or elicit from students, examples of the target items in use.
- If students are commonly making a mistake based on L1 interference, show them what the difference is between the two languages that produces the mistake: it will help them avoid it.
- If students can understand most of the content of what you are talking about – for example, when you're telling a story – allow yourself to translate an unknown word here and there, to help students follow.

Invite short responses

> Very often, you'll know students are understanding you as
> you speak through their eye-contact, facial expression and
> body language. But it's a good idea sometimes to do teacher
> talk-based activities that require brief or silent responses.

What I'm talking about here is listening comprehension activities based
on teacher talk that have students responding through some action or
a quick spoken word or two. But still, most of the time is taken up by
your own speech, with short pauses that allow students to respond.

So for example:

- Commands. Tell the students to do some action ('Put your hand on
  your head'): they do as you say.
  - Or: They do it only if you say 'please'.
  - Or: Tell them to do something while you yourself sometimes carry
    out the action and sometimes do something different. For example,
    you might say 'point to the door' and actually point to the window.
    They have to do what you say, not (necessarily) what you do.
- True/false. Make statements that are true or false: students nod if
  they are true, shake their heads if they are false.
- Catch me out. Tell a story, but every now and then say something
  obviously wrong or false. The students raise their hands if they hear
  such a mistake.
- Picture dictation. Describe an imaginary picture, of a landscape, for
  example, or person, or monster, and ask students to draw it
- Interrupt me. Tell a story: the students interrupt you to ask questions
  about what you've just said, which you have to answer. Or 'Correct me':
  tell a well-known story but add mistakes. The students have to correct.
- Note-taking. Give a talk, and ask students to take notes. If this is
  based on a text rather than improvised speech, then the talk can be
  expanded to a mixed-skills 'dicto-gloss' activity, where students try
  in groups to reconstruct the original text on the basis of their notes.

Testing and Assessment

Assessment is the part of teaching I enjoy least: but it's essential. Within the course, you do it so that you and the students can be aware of how you and they are doing, and what needs further work. And at the beginning or end of the course, it's done for external reasons: for placement in an appropriate level class, as a basis for formal certification, for employment, and so on.

Assess not only through tests 83

> Tests are useful tools for assessment, but they aren't the only ones, and may disadvantage students with test anxiety. Try to supplement tests with other means of assessment that are based on ongoing or periodic evaluations.

Tests as an assessment tool are convenient to administer, usually straightforward to check and grade and provide a single clear result. They will therefore probably continue to be used in most institutions, and in most contexts where the stakeholders (an education authority or the institution, for example) require a clear – usually numerical – assessment of how good at English a particular student is. They're also used to support ongoing teaching (*formative assessment*): to find out what students know and don't know at a particular point. The main aim in this case is to raise both students' and teachers' awareness of the students' level, and to help the teacher decide what needs to be focused on in the future.

They do, however, have disadvantages which we need to be aware of. For example, the test itself may not be well designed, and may not give reliable results; students with test anxiety may under-perform; any specific test may or may not include language that the students happen to know, or topics they are familiar with.

So use other sources of evaluation as well, preferably ones that enable you to check students' performance periodically as the course goes on rather than only at a single point. For example:

- Note down for yourself occasionally your impression of the classroom performance of individual students. It only takes a minute or two on your computer at the end of the day. Over time you'll find that you've made notes on most of them.
- Require students to gather their ongoing class or home assignments into a portfolio.
- Keep a record of homework assignments (see Tip 45).
- Ask students to self-assess (see Tip 84).

84 | Use (also) student self-assessment

> Self-assessment is a useful supplementary tool for evaluating student performance. It doesn't replace other tools, but provides information that can contribute to a more reliable overall grade.

Obviously, you wouldn't want to base a grade entirely on students' self-assessment, as it's difficult or impossible for them to be objective about their own performance. It's probable that the students themselves would not wish this. I once asked a (teenage, intermediate-level) class if they'd like to base their final grade on their own self-evaluations, and received a unanimous negative.

However, self-assessment can be very helpful as an added source of information. I frequently administered a questionnaire towards the end of a course, asking students various questions relating to their own learning. (With lower-level classes this was done in mother tongue.)

- What overall grade do you think you deserve?
- What do you think you are particularly good at in English?
- What do you feel you are not good at and need to work on?
- Do you feel you have worked well during this course?
- Do you think you have made progress since the beginning of this course? yes, a lot / quite a lot / a bit / not much

What I found really helpful and informative was the private discussions I held with individual students after they had filled in and submitted these questionnaires. You may not have the time to hold such sessions; but if you can, do. It's an opportunity to compare the grade you gave with the one they gave themselves (their self-assessment is often, surprisingly, lower than yours!), and discuss issues arising from their answers to other questions.

Your own assessment of a student may be changed a bit, or simply confirmed, by students' opinions of their own performance. But either way, it can contribute to the reliability of their final grades.

Use tests as a teaching tool

> Tests are normally seen simply as a tool for assessment. But actually periodical class tests administered by the teacher can contribute a lot to ongoing learning.

Many procedures called 'tests' in ongoing teaching are not in fact really testing anything: their main object is not to find out if students know something or not, but to enhance learning of the material. They are called tests partly because they get a grade, but mainly because this title raises their prestige, as it were, and students are more motivated to try to succeed in them.

Your main aim here is to get the students to learn the material thoroughly. The message you want to convey is 'This is a test, but I really want you to do well on it'. So if it's on a set of vocabulary items, for example, or a grammatical feature, tell the students what language items the test is going to include, and what sort of questions will be asked, and give plenty of class- and homework time to review the relevant material in advance. The test items themselves will give added opportunity for review. So will later checking: after you've marked the test, spend some of the following lesson on further discussion of any items that students found difficult.

A secondary aim is the feeling of closure. This type of test is often given at the end of a coursebook unit (or indeed at the end of learning of any particular chunk of material), and signals the closing of that unit and the expectation that we'll now move onto the next. It contributes to a general sense of structure and progress in the course.

Later, of course, the grades given on a number of such tests can also provide a useful contributor to overall student assessment.

86 Add optional sections to tests

> If you are composing your own tests for classroom use, it
> is a useful strategy to add extra sections that are optional
> and earn bonus points.

One of the problems of class tests is that the more advanced, or faster-
working, students, tend to finish early, and then you need to tell them
what to do next. Get on with homework? Read? Leave the class? The
slight noise that accompanies such events, even if it involves only two
or three members of the class, is also disturbing for those who are still
working. And the fact that some students have finished can be stressful
for those who are still struggling, perhaps only halfway through.

These problems can be solved by adding an extra optional section or
two to the test, and making it clear from the beginning, when you give
instructions, that anyone who finishes the main (compulsory) body
of the test before time is up should continue to the optional part. (See
some notes on this strategy applied to classroom activities in general for
heterogeneous classes, in Tip 42.)

Any student who completes some or all of the optional part should be
awarded 'bonus' points. I usually allow up to 20% more. Of course,
this can lead to some students getting grades like 112%, but if this is an
internal test, then who cares? The students certainly won't, and they will
appreciate the credit for extra effort.

The extra component should be something challenging and if possible
fun, not just more of the same. It could be a story to write, a crossword
puzzle to solve, a problem to discuss in writing, a letter to answer, a
picture to describe or comment on, a challenge to find as many answers
to a given question as they can.

Prepare students for the test 87

Preparing students carefully for a test not only helps them do better; it also goes some way towards relieving the problems of those who suffer from test anxiety.

If the test is a public, high-stakes examination then normally students know when it is going to be, and have the possibility of looking at previous papers to see how long they are, what sort of questions are asked and what the level of the language is.

If it's a teacher-prepared test, then the same kind of preparation should be made available. I dislike 'surprise tests / quizzes' when the students are suddenly faced with a test situation without any preparation: these only raise stress and do little or nothing for learning.

So make sure your students know in advance when the test will take place, more or less the kind of language they will be tested on – a specified set of items, or proficiency in general – and what is required of them in the different sections of the paper.

A few tips on test-taking can also help, such as:

- Read through the whole paper before you start.
- Do the questions you're sure you can answer first, then go back to the ones that are more difficult.
- Look through the comprehension questions before you read / listen to the text.

Note that it's not a good idea, if your students are preparing for a high-stakes public exam, to spend weeks and weeks beforehand just doing test papers. I know a lot of teachers who do this, but it doesn't help much, is boring, and may raise, rather than lower, stress. It's enough to allow students to rehearse the test a week or two before by doing two or three similar papers, timing themselves to get a sense of the speed they'll need to work, but with you available to help if needed.

88 Assess yourself

> Assessing is not just something you do to students; it's something you should be doing to yourself from time to time.

If you want to assess how well you are doing as a teacher, there are three kinds of people you can ask: colleagues; yourself; and your students.

Colleagues will only be able to give you reliable feedback on your teaching if they've observed you. It demands quite a lot of confidence and initiative to look for a sympathetic colleague who has the time and willingness to observe you and then give feedback – perhaps in return for your doing the same for him or her. It can be really helpful; but few of us manage it, particularly if we have a busy teaching schedule.

You yourself are a more accessible, if less objective, judge. The most important criteria are how well you feel your students are learning, and how motivated they are to come to lessons. Try not to be tempted to compare yourself to colleagues. If your lessons are less well-managed than those of colleague X, or if you can't act or tell jokes as well as colleague Y, this doesn't mean you are less good a teacher, just that your teaching style and personality are different.

But in my experience the best source of feedback and assessment is the students. They're the ones who know you best and can give you the most reliable information. Give them questionnaires from time to time, perhaps a couple of questions added to the self-assessment ones suggested in Tip 84. Don't make these too personal. (Don't ask 'What do you think of me as a teacher?'!) Ones I have used are: 'What in our lessons particularly helps you learn?', 'What do you feel doesn't help you learn?' or 'Can you suggest some ways the lessons could be improved and help you to learn better?'.

Vocabulary Teaching

The importance of vocabulary teaching is generally recognized these days, and there's been a lot of research on how best to teach it. This section includes some references to key studies.

89 Teach a lot of vocabulary
90 Teach multi-word chunks
91 Sometimes teach out of context
92 Do plenty of review
93 Use mother tongue to explain

89 **Teach a lot of vocabulary**

> Vocabulary is the most important thing to teach: you can't even begin to express yourself without knowing the forms and meanings of words.

When I started teaching I was told: 'Don't bother about teaching vocabulary, they'll pick it up, grammatical patterns are the priority' (this was the heyday of audiolingualism).

Big mistake! Huge!

It's essential to teach a lot of vocabulary in class as soon as possible. You need grammar, of course, as well – I'm not saying don't teach grammar. But much more time should be devoted to deliberate vocabulary teaching and review: I'd say about a third of lesson time in elementary and intermediate classes and not much less in advanced ones.

It appears that a large *sight vocabulary* (words you can immediately and automatically understand when you see them) is the main condition for successful reading comprehension. Grammar, background knowledge and reading strategies are less important. Vocabulary is also the basis of listening comprehension, and, of course, of speaking and writing.

The size of vocabulary needed for reading and understanding unsimplified texts has been estimated as something like 8,000 words (see the reference below). That's an enormous number, difficult to grasp. Let me put it like this: assuming an academic year of about 30 weeks, it means learning at least 30 words a week for eight years. And that doesn't take into account the learning of lexical chunks (see Tip 90) and the need for review (see Tip 92).

You can't expect students just to pick up all this vocabulary from their reading. Incidental learning of vocabulary from reading happens of course, but it's relatively slow, and most students in English courses simply don't read enough to enable them to reach the levels of knowledge indicated above. We need to teach vocabulary in class.

Schmitt, N. (2008). Instructed second language vocabulary learning. *Language Teaching Research*, *12(3)*, 329–363.

A lot of the vocabulary our students need is not single words, but multi-word chunks like *of course, by the way, take place.*

These are referred to in the literature by a variety of terms: formulaic expressions, idioms, prefabricated phrases, phrasal expressions, lexical chunks. I'll just use *chunks*.

The point about chunks is that they are learnt as single units, and retrieved from memory all at once, without the need for working out which word comes next according to a grammatical rule. So even sentences like *I don't know* are chunks in this sense.

But ones like *I don't know* are less essential to teach because you can deduce their meaning from the single words that are used in it, if you know the grammar. What it's really important to teach students is those chunks that they couldn't work out by themselves by knowing the single component words. For example, *by and large* means 'in general' but there's no way a learner could understand this meaning on the basis of knowledge of the single words *by, and, large.* (See the reference below for more examples.)

An important set of chunks are phrasal verbs like *look for, put up with*: their meaning is often very distant from the core meaning of the verb and the added preposition or adverb doesn't help very much.

A lot of coursebooks don't pay enough attention to these items when listing vocabulary to be learnt from a text. So it's a good idea to go through any text you're planning to read and pick out(!) any useful chunks that you're going to want to teach, as well as the obvious single words.

Try doing this with the text on this page!

Martinez, R., & Schmitt, N. (2012). A phrasal expressions list. *Applied Linguistics*, 33(3), 299–320.

Sometimes teach out of context

> In general, it's a good principle to teach vocabulary in
> context. But there are situations where you can – and
> should – focus on an item in isolation.

If you learn a new vocabulary item in a context, then you are likely to
become familiar with how it connects with other words, how it works
grammatically, and in what kinds of texts it's likely to appear. All this
is important. But it can also help to focus on the item on its own as a
target for learning in its own right.

One such place is the first encounter with a new item. If you write
the item on its own on the board, and pronounce it clearly, as well
as explaining or translating it, the students are far more likely to pay
attention to it and learn it than if its meaning is just noted in context.
It's a question of impact: the impact a new item makes on learners
when it is first learnt makes a big difference as to how well it will be
remembered. Normally, in order to make such an impact the item has to
be 'foregrounded', and perceived on its own separate from its original
context. Such impact can be enhanced if you use a picture, or mime, or
a *mnemonic device* (memory aid) like an imaginative link to a word in
the students' mother tongue.

Later, you might want to enrich and deepen your students' knowledge
of the new word: what other words it tends to go with (collocations);
what idioms or expressions it is part of; what other meanings it can
have; whether it can be used as another part of speech; what other
words mean the same sort of thing, or the opposite. A good exercise
here is to ask students to look up the word in a dictionary and find out
more information about it.

Finally, there is a good case for basing some of the vocabulary review
exercises on decontextualized items (see Tip 92).

Do plenty of review

> **It's virtually impossible to learn a vocabulary item from a single encounter. Normally you need to review it several times to make sure it's permanently remembered.**

Learners probably have to review a new vocabulary item between ten and sixteen times to ensure it is learned (see the reference below). Some opportunities for review will be provided by incidental encounters within texts or interaction; but the more advanced the item is, the more unlikely it is that it will be re-encountered by chance. For example, supposing you've just taught some intermediate students the word *leaf*. How likely is it that they'll come across it again by chance within the next few days?

This means that once you've taught a new item, you have to create opportunities for focused review. Of course, you're not going to have time to review every new item six, let alone sixteen, times in lessons, but you certainly need to do so at least three or four times and hope that the extra encounters will over time be supplied by students' reading or listening outside the classroom.

Because of time constraints, it makes sense to have most review based on quick tasks that get the students to retrieve the meaning or form of the items, without a surrounding sentence context. As soon as you start contextualizing within sentences or short texts, the exercise becomes much more time-consuming.

Some examples:

- Challenge students to remember all the new items you've taught over the last two weeks: write them up on the board as fast as they say them, and remind them of meanings where necessary.
- Write up the items you want to review. Students ask about any they don't remember.
- Dictate the items in mother tongue. Students write them down in English (or vice versa).

Zahar, R, T. Cobb & N. Spada. (2001). Acquiring vocabulary through reading: effects of frequency and contextual richness. *Canadian Modern Language Review* , 57(4), 544–72.

93 Use mother tongue to explain

> There are lots of ways we use to explain meanings of new words: mother-tongue (L1) translation is probably the single most efficient one.

Translation can only be used, of course, if your students share a mother tongue which you also know; but this is the situation in most classrooms worldwide.

L1 in English teaching is a good deal more widely used these days than it used to be (see the reference below), though it's still frowned on by some. Explaining new vocabulary is one key use, for various reasons:

- It's much quicker than an explanation in English.
- It's much more easily understood.
- It usually gives a pretty accurate idea of the meaning of the item.

I know it's happened to me more than once that after I'd carefully explained a new word in English, one of my students called out the L1 translation ... and everyone breathed a sigh of relief! And students on the whole like to know what the L1 equivalent is even if they understand the English explanation: ask them.

This does not, of course, mean that you should abandon other methods of clarifying meaning: explanations, synonyms, examples, pictures, mime and gesture, contrast with opposites and so on. These are helpful in supplying more information, interest and impact and will help students remember the new item. The problem is that they may not always be understood correctly and some of them are rather time-consuming. In many cases it's probably best either to use one or more of such strategies backed up with a quick translation later to make sure the meaning is clear; or first translate and then add your explanations, examples and so on, knowing that all these will now be understood. Extra explanation is also useful as clarification if there are significant differences in meaning and/or use between the English and the L1 translation.

Kerr, P. (2014). *Translation and own-language activities*. Cambridge: Cambridge University Press.

Writing

Writing has become a much more important skill in recent years owing to the increase in the use of digital communications like email, SMS, blogging and so on. So we need to enable our students to compose not only formal prose but also informal messages – and to be aware of the differences.

Use copying tasks for beginners

> For beginner learners whose own language does not use
> the Latin script, copying can be a very useful activity,
> provided they know the sounds or meanings of what they
> are copying.

Handwriting will continue to be important for the foreseeable future, in
spite of the growing use of computer keyboards. Beginner students need
to learn how to write the letters themselves: a challenge particularly for
those whose mother tongue does not use the Latin alphabet, and may
not even be read from left to right.

Having been taught the shapes and sounds of the letters, students
need practice in writing them. At this stage, copying tasks are useful
because they give this practice, while freeing the writer of the need to
retrieve the new forms entirely from memory. However, copying tasks
can be boring, and there's not much point being able to draw a letter
if you don't know what it sounds like! So the tasks should be designed
to require at least knowledge of the sound, if not meaning, of what is
being copied.

Some possible tasks are the following:

- Students copy each letter and write next to it the mother-tongue
  letter that sounds similar.
- There is a set of letters or words on the board and students copy
  down the ones the teacher says.
- There is a set of letters (e.g. *b, a, l, c, h*) next to a picture representing
  a known word (e.g. a drawing of an apple) and students copy only
  those letters whose sound appears in the word.
- There is a set of words next to a picture and students copy only
  those words that are relevant to the picture.
- Students copy a set of names of people and; write next to each *m* (if
  it's a male name) or *f* (if female).
- Students copy a word and draw a picture representing it.

Writing assignments are normally done for homework, but it's also useful to do some in-class writing activities.

I'm not talking here about writing done in the course of routine procedures, such as noting down new words or grammar, or the answers to comprehension or grammar exercises, but about tasks done for the sake of improving the writing skills themselves.

Writing takes much more time than the other three skills of listening, speaking and reading, particularly for learners at the early stages who may write very slowly. Later, longer writing tasks demand careful thought and reflection so most people prefer to write quietly on their own at home. For these reasons, most writing will probably be done for homework.

However, the advantage of giving writing assignments in class is that you, the teacher, are there to provide support and immediate feedback. You can help with vocabulary and spelling and you have a chance to see and correct mistakes immediately or approve successful composition. So give in-class writing occasionally, at all levels.

It's best if you define the activity by time rather than quantity (see Tip 41). That way students keep writing all the time until you stop them, and you don't need to worry about those who finish early or late.

Some ideas:

- A set of brief elementary writing tasks: see those suggested in Tip 94.
- Five-minute writing storms: give students a topic and five minutes to write as much as they can about it.
- A set of beginnings of sentences: students write as many different endings for each as they can think of.
- Chain writing: each student writes the first sentence of a story or a poem at the top of a piece of paper and passes it to a neighbour, who writes the next sentence and so on.

Students can share their compositions later by reading them aloud or by exchanging them between themselves. You can also read out some of them (with the writers' permission!).

> English spelling is not as difficult as it is popularly
> assumed to be; but students do need to know the basic
> rules in order to be able to spell correctly.

Take any page of the dictionary, and go through the words in it, noting
how many of them are irregular: that means they do not accord with
spelling rules like the 'magic *e*' (see the first rule in the list below), or the
spelling of the *-tion* ending. You'll probably find that more than 85% of
them are regular. Most English words are spelt according to rules that
are easy to teach and learn and enable students to spell most new words
accurately. So don't face students with defeatist statements like 'English
spelling is very difficult', but tell them rather: 'You can spell most
English words correctly if you learn the rules'.

The problem is, of course, that it's the most common words that are
genuinely irregular: words like *what, are, who, would,* which need to be
taught one at a time. But most words accord with spelling rules. Here
are some I've found useful:

- An *e* at the end of a word makes the preceding vowel sound like its
  name (e.g. *make*).
- The sound /s/ is usually spelt *s*, but may be *c* if there's an *i* or *e* after
  it (e.g. *nice*).
- The sound /ʃən/ at the end of a word is usually spelt *tion* (e.g. *nation*).
- The sound /k/ at the end of a short word is usually spelt *ck* (e.g. *back*).
- The sound /l/ at the end of a short word is usually spelt *ll* (e.g. *tall*).
- The sound /l/ at the end of a long word is usually spelt *l* (e.g. *usual*).
- The sound /i:/ at the end of a word is usually spelt *y* (e.g. *happy*).
- When *all* is at the beginning of a word, it is usually spelt with one *l*
  (e.g. *always*).

You can probably add more.

Encourage typing

> Handwriting is of course needed as a basic skill; but knowing how to type fast is essential these days when most extended writing is done through the computer keyboard.

One of the courses that most benefited my future career as an English teacher (and later as a writer) was one I took years ago in touch-typing using an old-fashioned typewriter. Most teachers don't touch-type. This is mainly, perhaps, because it doesn't seem necessary: they feel they type adequately without touch-typing, and certainly at the beginning it slows you down. But eventually, when you get good at it, being able to touch-type makes a huge difference to the fluency and sheer speed of keyboard-based writing, which is the kind of writing most of us do most of the time. No 'hunt and peck' typing can ever be as fast as touch-typing, and it frees your eyes to check what is coming up on the screen as you write.

So do yourself a favour and teach yourself to touch-type, using one of the many online courses available; and encourage your students to do the same. It's worth it even if your local keyboard is slightly different in layout from the British/American 'QWERTY' one.

In any case, get your students to type most of their written assignments, and to submit them to you in digital form, if the technology is available. This can be done through email attachment. If you are using a Learning Management System (LMS) like *Moodle* then it's even easier. Getting students to write their assignments using computer word-processing software is a good investment, as they are likely to do most of their writing in this way in the future. It also makes dealing with the assignments much easier from your point of view. You can correct and comment on them on screen, return them immediately, and then keep them in easily-retrieved folders for future reference.

Get students to rewrite

At the more advanced levels, get students to redraft their written compositions two or three times in response to your feedback before finalizing them.

Drafting and redrafting in response to feedback (*process writing*), is the best way to get more advanced students to improve their writing. This applies to many kinds of writing: an academic essay, for example, a story, a web page, a formal letter or email. For one thing, it ensures that any corrective feedback is in fact taken on board and implemented. If they didn't have to rewrite, many students might not even pay attention to your corrections, let alone internalize them. For another, it accustoms students to the idea of rereading their own compositions with a critical eye and rewriting, which is essential if they are to become good writers. And it is authentic: it is the process any professional writer goes through on the way to publication.

Don't give your students a grade on the first draft, but delay assessment until after they have rewritten the text a couple of times, and preferably only when they themselves feel it is ready. Not giving students a grade on the first draft has further advantages. It encourages them to take risks and use all the language at their disposal when composing, even if they're not sure it's correct, because they know they won't be penalized.

Students will be more motivated to revise their writing if the final product is to be published, and it's a good idea to find ways of publishing to a wider readership. In some classes, finished products can be displayed on the wall; in others, a class magazine or a collection in the form of a booklet can be published either in paper or digital form. Potential readers may be limited to the members of the class itself, or it may be widened to include other classes in the school, the parents, or if it's on the internet in an open website, an unlimited audience.

Most of our students these days have mobile phones which they use for texting in their mother tongue. They can also use them for writing in English.

Some teachers ban the use of mobile phones in the classroom, but why not use them for writing (and reading) practice? It's an appealing and fun way to get students to write for real communication. Many of my teacher colleagues have downloaded a popular app which enables a number of people to be included in a sort of group texting programme: a text message sent by one of them can be seen and responded to by all. They list all the students in a class, and then can easily give information to the entire group, as well as engage with other kinds of informal interactions with students; questions and answers, exchange of news, jokes, and so on.

But even through one-to-one interactions, mobile phones can be used to practise writing. You need first to make sure that each student has everyone else's number on their 'contacts' list. (This in itself is a fun 'milling' activity that practises numbers: students walk around asking for and noting down each other's numbers.)

Then try asking students to do things like the following:

- Send each other 'getting to know you' questions, like 'Do you have any brothers or sisters?' and respond (a good 'ice-breaker').
- Send each other opinion questions: 'What do you think of...?' and respond.
- Quiz each other about new words they've learnt recently: 'What does ... mean?'.

A linked activity is to look at a sample of SMS text and compare it with formal conventional writing: what are the differences? Most students know perfectly well that they shouldn't use texting conventions like smileys or abbreviations like *fyi* or *asap*, or *u* for *you* in normal essay writing, but it's useful to raise awareness of these and other differences.

P.S.

100   Do your own thing

> To be really good at teaching you need to find your own
> teaching style and choose the methodology that suits you
> and your students.

Your main source of expertise has to be your own experience and
experimenting – the more the better – supplemented by student
feedback and discussion with colleagues or interaction with other
teachers at conferences or online.

The next best source is the expertise of others, whether practitioners
or academics, which you get through books and articles, websites
(particularly blogs), conferences and in-service courses. The trouble
is that there's an enormous amount of stuff out there. And there's no
way any of us can gain access to all, or even most, of it, we're too busy
teaching. But do try to read, or hear, as much as you can. Conferences
and teachers' workshops, whether local or international, are particularly
refreshing – and fun! – and a great place to get ideas from other
professionals, or thought-provoking insights from the research.

And then rely on your own critical judgement as to which ideas from
all this input are right for you. Don't let the 'experts' tell you what's best
for your classroom: you're the only one who knows. Listen to what they
have to say, read what they have written, consider it carefully. And then
decide for yourself whether you agree or not, and which of their ideas are
right for you, will help your students learn better, and can contribute to
your own expertise. (The same applies, of course, to the tips in this book.)

The first tip in this book was 'start with a smile'. I hope that reading
this last one will also leave you with a 'smiley' feeling! Because teaching
should be fun and enjoyable for you as well as successful in terms of
getting your students to learn English. And doing your own thing is the
best way to achieve both.

Index

Photo Acknowledgements

The authors and publishers acknowledge the following sources of copyright material and are grateful for the permissions granted. While every effort has been made, it has not always been possible to identify the sources of all the material used, or to trace all copyright holders. If any omissions are brought to our notice, we will be happy to include the appropriate acknowledgements on reprinting and in the next update to the digital edition, as applicable.

Back cover photograph by Yair Ur.

Printed in the United States
By Bookmasters